Running Around In Family Circles with Friends in Pursuit

Georgia Griffith

Copyright © 2003 by Georgia Griffith

Running Around In Family Circles with Friends in Pursuit
by Georgia Griffith

Printed in the United States of America

ISBN 1-594670-36-6

All rights reserved. No part of this publication may be reproduced or transmitted in any form or by any means without written permission of the author.

Xulon Press
www.XulonPress.com

Xulon Press books are available in bookstores everywhere, and on the Web at www.XulonPress.com.

Dedication

To my family and friends
with
laughter, love, and tears

Acknowledgments

Grateful thanks are extended to my friend and editor,
Dr. Bob Solomon of Canada for editing the submission copy.

To Howard and David Goldstein for suggestions about technology

To Carol Roper for research and general assistance

To my family and friends for permission to use their material.

CHAPTER 1

Georgia, Handicapped, Impaired, Challenged, and Then a Wizard.

I am the only blind person in my family we know of, except for one of Grandpa Moore's Brothers, who developed vision problems from diabetes, at an advanced age. I was born blind and when I started to school, I learned that I was not blind after all, just "visually handicapped". A few years later I was told that I was "visually impaired". Now I find out am "visually challenged" and, of course, I still can't see one bit better. No matter what it is called, not being able to see is the same thing, and for those who find themselves named "handicapped", "impaired, or "challenged" in any way, how we adjust to whatever we are makes all the difference to our lives.

One of my first childhood memories is of a lady who came to talk with my family about sending me to the State School for the Blind. Back then there was no other choice for us, there were no integrated classes in public schools. My father did not want me to leave, and neither did my mother, but she recognized the value of education and, with an aching heart, she agreed to let me try classes for six weeks in the spring after I was five years old. It was hoped that this "kindergarten-like" period before then would help me adjust to being away from home for the first time in my life.

Braille alphabet.

After I survived this brief period of my first official schooling, the authorities wanted me to skip a few grades but my mother, always wise about these things, believed I was already the youngest in the class and skipping me ahead by months and even years might cause problems with my older (and bigger) peers. To keep me busy and interested, the school tried something quite inventive and started me on piano lessons. It worked and music has always been a big part of my life. I can still play the piano although, having become deaf (or handicapped, impaired, challenged, and a Wizard), I can no longer hear it. How we adjust makes all the difference again.

I attended that state school all the way through high school and then enrolled in regular classes at Capital University in Columbus, Ohio. I was the first blind student ever to enter regular classes there. I adjusted, the school adjusted to having me there, and friends helped every second, every year. I have always recognized that behind every successful person stand hundreds of unsung heroes who have given their time and their efforts with no awards. Many of these people are introduced to you in this book. When I was a fresh-

Running Around In Family Circles with Friends in Pursuit

man at Capital my roommate, Jeanne Ellis, learned to write Braille so she could record the things I needed to keep. We had no machines to help us in those days and each Braille dot had to be embossed separately. Like Middle Eastern languages, Braille was written from right to left and each character was formed in reverse so it would appear on the other side of the paper in the proper shape. Some people liked to describe our special way of writing as mirror writing with invisible ink. Jeanne adjusted herself to this magical gift for me, her new friend.

Jeanne Ellis married after her sophomore (my freshman) year. Her husband always signed his name "your roommate-in-law". Robert Graetz has been a successful minister for all the years since those college days. He certainly adjusted to our magical friendship. My adjustment was helped by my own good luck as well as by my good companions. I am thankful I was blessed with a good memory and did not need to record large amounts of text, Still, all my notes in college were embossed manually. Today, decades after we embossed and laughed together, Bob and Jeanne live about an hour's drive from here and when they are in town they sometimes stop to visit for a little while.

The following speech was given to the audience by Bettye Krolick when I received the Fred Sinclair Award from the California Transcribers and Educators of the Visually Handicapped. After the time outlined in the speech, I received a number of awards including DAR (Daughters of the American Revolution), Smithsonian Medal, Sertoma (Service To Mankind), The Great Communicator, The Ohio Women's Hall of Fame, and in 1974, I received the Capital University Alumni Achievement Award and a chair. Some friends asked what it meant to receive a chair, and with tongue in cheek I explained to them, as patiently as possible, how to sit down in a chair and rest after all your work was finished. It really is a wooden chair, complete with arms and a plaque on the back. Life has certainly not been empty.

Here, while I blush (I think!) is the speech:

Tribute to Georgia Griffith

By Bettye Krolick

Talented artists are sometimes described as having different stages of life. This was his "blue" period or that was his "pointillistic" period. CTEVH (California Transcribers and Educators of The Visually Handicapped) has a life member who is an artist of many talents and whose life, so far, has three distinct periods. I am speaking of Georgia Griffith who did not know she is to be honored tonight and who is just now reading in Braille what I am telling you. The problem is, of course, that she can read faster than I can speak. Slow down, Georgia!

For information on Georgia's life I went to the American Biographical Institute volume titled, "Two Thousand Notable American Women", where Georgia Griffith is rightfully listed. According to this she was born in 1931 and graduated in 1954 with a B.A. in Music Education. When Georgia submitted this material she left out the fact that as the first blind person to attend Capital University she graduated Phi Beta Kappa Cum Laude. It lists her occupation 1954-1970 as Music Instructor. Yes, and she also helped with the visually impaired students at the local public school. This first period of her life was as a successful blind person. But a few years before 1970 Georgia could no longer earn a living as a music instructor. Her wonderful ears had gone deaf, she was paralyzed on one side, and she was struggling not only to become physically rehabilitated but also to find a purpose for living.

The second period of Georgia's life was the blind-deaf period and the biographical listing states, "Braille Music Proofreader, Library of Congress, 1971-1989." Georgia had learned a new profession. She had her literary and music certifications, and, as is characteristic, Georgia was and is the only Class A certified Braille music proof reader.

Georgia had also adopted a motto for her life: "To Give is to Live." She purchased a Xerox machine for her tiny home office and she also obtained a thermoform machine. That wouldn't fit in the office, so it squeezed into her bedroom. With that equipment she

Running Around In Family Circles with Friends in Pursuit

started giving the music transcribers of California and every other state extra help. When we goofed, she would Xerox the print and thermoform the Braille information that would help us do better next time. Georgia's motto was alive and active.

Here is part of a letter Elinor Savage quickly sent me when I told her about tonight's honor. "Georgia has always been an endless source of support and knowledge - I wouldn't trust anyone else to answer my many questions about music Braille - answers that always come by return mail. Her never-ending vitality, impressive intelligence, and sense of humor have kept me her most ardent admirer for many years."

During the mid-1970s I was writing a dictionary of Braille music signs for NLS (National Library Service). This was when her Phi Beta Kappa brain really showed its stuff. When I would receive information in Braille in a foreign language - any foreign language, Georgia would say, no problem, I can translate it. She would immediately start learning that language! She taught herself 12 or 13 foreign languages during that period in order to translate entire books about Braille music so that I would have the information for the dictionary. She did this entirely as a volunteer. To Give is to Live.

The transition from this period to the next started at a CTEVH Conference, and I believe it was in March of 1980. In the exhibits there was something called a VersaBraille. With her intelligence Georgia realized what it could do for her, so she placed an order. She did not have the $5,000 purchase price, but she told me they were still just being manufactured and TSI could not fill the order until fall which would give her time to do a lot of extra paid proofreading for Texas and other places as well as NLS.

The proofreading work was actually very slow that summer, so I talked my bank into setting up an account to receive money to be used for Georgia Griffith. I sent a short letter to about 75 music Braillists most of whom I had never met. I explained that she was our proofreader, that she had ordered a VersaBraille she could not afford, and I told something about what it might do for her. I said this would be a complete surprise to Georgia but any money that was donated would help towards purchasing the VersaBraille. I explained that it was not necessary to write a letter; checks could simply be sent directly to that bank account.

I was amazed. I received many letters with checks enclosed. They all thanked me for presenting the opportunity to do something for Georgia who had done so much for them. All $5,000 was raised within one month.

So this launched Georgia into the third period, which I call the "Electronic Wizard" period of her life.

The VersaBraille arrived early in 1981. Georgia knew nothing about computers, but she learned fast. Joining a computer hobbyist service called CompuServe allowed her to read a newspaper directly for the first time, to have access to all sorts of information and best of all to communicate via the computer with people from all walks of life and from all parts of the United States. With the computer no one could tell that she was either blind or deaf.

In March of 1981 Georgia was back at CTEVH giving her first demonstration on how to use this instrument. David Usland was the workshop leader and very few people attended. They had no idea at that time how electronics would impact the lives of transcribers, teachers and the visually impaired.

Soon Georgia had a part-time job as an Information Specialist on Compuserve but she was not content just to soak up all the information and friendships she now had access to. She decided CompuServe should have a database for the handicapped. She took the proposal to the company and they gave her space online in the services. She built a wonderful data base. Not just for the visually impaired, it serves all handicaps. She provides an opportunity for people to ask questions on the computer service, and no matter what the question, she finds the answers.

Lets go back to the biographical listing at this point: "Database Manager, CompuServe, Inc. 1982 to the present; Information Specialist, LINC Resources, Inc., 1986 to the present; Board of Directors, National Braille Association, 1981- 1987; Board of Directors, Center for Special Education Technology, 1984-1987" (this is part of CEC, Council for Exceptional Children). "Computer operator, National Policies and Issues Forum, 1982 to the present, and IBM/Special Needs Exchange, 1987 to the present," and today she is a Forum Manager on CompuServe with an official title of

Running Around In Family Circles with Friends in Pursuit

"Wizard!" This is truly her electronic wizard period.

There is no possible way to estimate the number of lives Georgia Griffith has reached with her helping hands and her motto, "to Give is to Live." She helps people learn how to use computer equipment- adaptive or otherwise, she provides consolation when they come to her with problems concerning a handicapped child or relative. She is able to answer personal questions about living with the handicapped; questions people are embarrassed to ask face to face. On the computer it is impersonal, but they know she has had the experiences and will talk frankly with them.

During this 10-year period Georgia has continued to help music transcribers, she has continued to Give and to Live in so very many ways. Here is just one more example. When she was able to obtain a Kurzweil Reading Machine, she sent me a file online containing the first part of my dictionary of Braille music signs. She told me she had just used it to test out the Kurzweil. The next day another file arrived with the next portion of the dictionary. She said she was practicing with the controls and it was working better now. As the files continued to arrive I realized what she was doing. My dictionary was written in the 70s when I had no computer. Now I had been asked to make an international revision and add material to it. She knew that if I had the whole dictionary in my computer, it would be so much easier to make changes and expand it. So she didn't ask; she simply sent me the entire dictionary file by file. It took hours of valuable Kurzweil reading time, but she did it to help a friend.

Obviously I could go on and on, but it is time for Fred Sinclair to present Georgia Griffith with the prestigious Fred Sinclair Award for extraordinary service to the visually impaired and to a lot of other people besides.

CHAPTER 2

My immediate family: The warmest circle

My parents, Bernard Griffith and Florence Mae Moore, were married in 1928, just a year before the Great Depression. Life was difficult for many people during that time, and raising three small children in those years was a real accomplishment. My sister, Bernadine, was born in 1930, I joined the group in 1931 and my brother, John, appeared in 1933. Despite the difficult times my father bought a house for us and worked very hard to pay for it.

"Daddypop", as I called him when I was small, raised many of our vegetables in his garden, kept chickens to give us eggs, worked in a local factory and hauled coal after work at the factory to earn enough money to support us. "Daddypop" called me "Buttercup". I was a chubby little girl, but Daddy always said I was "nothing but skin and bones". My only memories of Daddy are early ones since he passed away in 1953, just six weeks before his 48th birthday. He was preparing his garden for spring planting when he suffered a massive heart attack.

My mother was a nurse and she was always helping with someone who was ill. Mother was a fun-loving person and she had many wise sayings and funny comments that she would insert into her conversations. We knew just about what she would say before she said it. When she was very happy about something she would announce "I'm so teakettled I can't coffeepot." When we children were too noisy she would say "Leave my share of that out" or "Can that!" She always claimed that Daddy was the head of the house but she was the neck and could turn the head any way she chose.

Mother Florence Mae Griffith- "Toots" - where all of this began.

Mother always made sure we were clean and our clothes were presentable. She and an aunt made most of my dresses and kept my clothes in good shape because, as I indicated in Chapter 1, I attended the Ohio State School for the Blind, which was a boarding school and did not have her daily help. All our clothes had to be marked with our names in indelible ink because they went to a common laundry and were then packaged for the person whose name was on them. The person who sorted clothes mated our socks, but in my case anyway, Mother told me the colors and I remembered them. She bought things with different textures that I could feel and told me their colors. I recall one dress that I just had to have. It had dots on it in the shape of a Braille g and I said this meant it was mine.

When I attended the school there were 200 students in all. Some were totally blind while others had enough vision to read large print. The latter were still "legally blind", and the rest of us joked about being "illegally blind". Some teachers, too, were blind, like Mr. Niday, our history and civics teacher. He told us of building a lovely doghouse for his dog in the basement and when he was finished and ready to take it outside he found it was too large to take through the door.

Other staff had full vision, like Mr. Meyer, our eighth grade teacher. I recall one class in which he asked "How many of you enjoy sports?" I was not too fond of sports then so I did not respond. Mr. Meyer then said, "I can line up 20 chairs, take off my shoes and jump over them." With a smile, I told him I could jump over my shoes with no sports training at all.

One time at the beginning of the school year our superintendent, Mr. Scarberry, announced that he had had an appendectomy in the summer and he read some of the cards he had received. The last one had us roaring with laughter; it was addressed to "Mr. Scarbelly." That name change seemed very appropriate and just right in a time when gangsters could be named "Scarface".

Over the years, my class, which was a rather large one, ranged from 15 to 20 students. I recall an incident when spelling and pronunciation caused an uproar of laughter. Shirley asked the teacher "What on earth is 'eggwiped'?" "How is it spelled?" asked the teacher. "E g y p t," replied Shirley. A little later another student was reading aloud and announced that "The woman admired the silverware hanging over the brassiere (brazier)". Laughter comes easily when you are young and make mistakes like these.

In the dormitory, five students were placed in almost every bedroom, with a locker for each one of us. A few rooms had space for only three people. Each student had a bed and a chair, and there was one table where we could study.

At the school, I also learned to cook, sew, weave, knit, crochet and weave baskets (really!). I had one pattern for a throw rug that had Indian figures in it. Their feet pointed toward each other and I turned one row of figures around so I could use the rug for a wall hanging. I did a lot of weaving of

Mary Alyce Doran in a dress Georgia knitted for her.

stand covers, and made the material for a skirt. I knotted afghans and sweaters for family and friends and even knitted a couple dresses for myself. Unfortunately, those dresses became smaller and smaller over the years and I finally gave them to a close friend who is still very thin. This training in crafts prepared me for a summer job during college days. I assisted Bernie at the local playgrounds teaching children simple crafts such as braiding strips of plastic.

The first sewing machines we used were the kind you had to pedal but later we obtained some electric models. When friends and neighbors visited us they were horrified to see me using the sewing machine. They were sure I would run the needle into my finger but I never did that. I was taught to be careful and, although I know several seeing people who were caught that way, I was never among them.

At home, I helped Mother with the ironing, too, and I remember one neighbor said "She'll burn herself." Mother replied "Then she won't do it that way again." Mother protected us where necessary but never over-protected us when we wanted to try something, and I wanted to learn to do my own ironing.

Of course, we also learned all the other subjects required by the State Department of Education for sighted children. We had a lot more music training than usually given in public schools, however. Anyone capable of playing an instrument was sent to Mr. Beckes, the school's band and orchestra director, and he taught us how to play as well as what to play. Mr. Beckes was a violinist in the Columbus Philharmonic Orchestra and he was the type of person everyone seems to enjoy.

We also had a chorus and learned to sing many of the great works, all by rote. We sang long and serious works like "The Messiah" and also some fun works. One song, full of advice, went like this:

> The more you study the more you know.
> The more you know the more you forget.
> The more you forget the less you know.
> So why study?

> The less you study the less you know.
> The less you know the less you forget.
> The less you forget the more you know.
> So why study?

There was also a junior chorus, little children who sang songs like "The Teddy Bears' Picnic". Our chorus sang on the radio a few times and at least once on TV.

During school days we often went on field trips, visiting such facilities as a firehouse, the penitentiary, where we sat in the electric chair, and many times to the zoo. When I was six years old I rode an elephant at the zoo and 50 years later when that elephant died, I was sorry to hear it. Thinking of elephants reminds me of a rather embarrassing time for me at school. Our science teacher had asked the class "What is a compound?" I raised my hand and with my tongue a little twisted I said "It is when two elephants (elements) are joined together." So many things, even elephants, live in one's memory.

One of the main events of our school years was Christmas with the Lions Club. Two months before Santa was expected, the Lions would ask each child for a first and second choice for what the child would like to have for Christmas. At the annual party Santa would call each child's name and sometimes make comments about things we were sure Santa could not know anything about, let alone be telling everyone. Santa would say "Let me hear the Lions roar," and the men would make as much noise as possible. Then he would want to hear the Lionesses roar and they tried to outdo the men. It was fun for all, even for Santa.

Christmas at home was a little different but just as much fun. We children would all join hands and go down the stairs together to see what Santa had brought. The family circle wound its way downstairs.

Memories stay, deep within us, even if we take a bit longer recalling them, but things change over time, and not always for the better. It is sad that the State school no longer offers instrumental music as part of the curriculum. but most of the students who attend the school now are children with multiple disabilities. Capable students attend integrated classes in the public schools. On the other hand, sometimes things get better, too. Some communities even have special schools for children with disabilities and it is wonderful that these special children can live at home and gather life-long memories as I did.

Mother spent many hours in the kitchen preparing food for us. One time she made a peach pie and did not have enough peaches to finish so she added apples to one side. We never let her live that down. Whenever she baked a peach pie we would ask where the apples were. When I cooked at home, I expected packages of ingredients to be where I had placed them. On one fine day, though, someone had moved things around and I added ingredients to the packaged cake frosting and baked that. What a mess I made that day!

Mother tried to teach Bernie to say a poem when she was two and a half years old. The session went like this:

    M: Roses on my shoulders
    B: Roses on my shoulders

    M: Slippers on my feet.
    B: Slippers on my feet

    M: I'm my mama's darling
    B: I'm my mama's darling

    M: Don't you think I'm sweet?
    B: Uh-huh.

Since Mother was so busy with household chores, my sister, Bernadine (Bernie), took me under her wing when I was home. Some people called her "The Little Mother". In these early days only one church here had vacation Bible school and Bernie and I attended that in the summer for several years. I learned a lot about the Bible and churches and we had a lot of fun singing kids' songs.

Bernie took me to play with other groups of children, helped me play baseball by putting my hand on the bat and swinging it for me and when we were older she helped me learn to ride a bicycle — all over the street, 'tis true, but I did it. When I was five years old, Bernie and I went to a meeting of the LTL (Loyal Temperance

League). They wanted me to sign a pledge never to drink liquor. "Liquor?" I had no idea what they were talking about so I said "I want one good taste first." Never got that, so, of course, I never signed the pledge.

Bernie liked to clean up the house and she was good at it but this left the rest of us hunting for the things she had put away when she was clearing our clutter. When she was a teenager she cleaned house for a couple of trusted, local families to earn a little pocket money. It wasn't a shame, it was work, and maybe even fun.

Bernie played clarinet in her high school marching band, and in 1948 that band took part in the filming of a horse racing movie called "The Green Grass of Wyoming." Most of that movie was filmed at our fairground and on the fiftieth anniversary of its filming, there was a rerun here and a number of historical articles about it. The movie was an oldie but it still seemed a work of art and Bernie loves art and enjoys working with pictures.

In my school days, I played the violin for a while in the school orchestra and then changed to horn before moving later to trumpet. My instrument-changes were necessary for the orchestra. They already had other students playing the violin, and the school needed someone to play horn and then someone for the trumpet. I was happy with all three, but I always said the strings sounded better inside the cat, anyway at least when I was the violin player.

I also played in the school band. We traveled around and played for other schools. There was very little Braille music then, and our director, Mr. Beckes, taught us a lot by rote. He directed the performances the same as he would have a seeing group but actually when we performed, he followed us. He started the number off by tapping his baton on the stand and we raised our instruments ready to play then he whispered "two three four" or whatever the count might be, and we started off together. After that he had little control over the number. For one performance, we practiced when he was at home with his family. Then at the concert, to his great surprise, we performed Sousa's "Our Director" in a very non-standard way. Some of us played accompaniment while the rest sang "Three cheers for our director, leader of the band; Here at the blind school he treats us man to man". Mr. Beckes told the audience he had no idea we were going to do that. Fun was part of everything we did, or we made it part. Even in the dark, I laugh.

In college days, a little more Braille music was available but I found a few transcribers who were willing to help supply things I needed. These transcribers were all volunteers who received no pay at all except our thanks. Braille music has become such a popular item today that transcribers now can charge for their work.

Students in the music education courses at Capital had to play one instrument from each group for a semester and three others for six weeks each so I played most of the instruments. My oboe sounded like a sick duck because I pinched the double reed. I am reminded of the time the oboe class was practicing "Silent Night" and the class next door ran out thinking it was a fire drill.

Equipment showing how writing braille progressed from manual to machine and then to computer..

After my graduation from college, Mother read music to me to transcribe so I could sing in the church choir. By then I had acquired a Perkins Brailler, which was a machine that allowed me to form letters and symbols right side up so that I could see at any moment what I had written. The characters were formed in one piece rather than one dot at a time. What an improvement! Before

Running Around In Family Circles with Friends in Pursuit

these machines were available, all embossing, except at printing houses where large embossing machines were used, had to be done manually with a slate and stylus, one dot at a time and in reverse so the characters could be read normally from left to right.

I directed the junior choir for some time and needed music for that project. The giggly teenagers were sometimes hard to control. I recall one Sunday when they sang and we had a guest, a retired minister. He was a little confused about what he was reading and instead of saying "God knoweth" he announced "God only knows." The teens giggled and laughed aloud at that. They liked wordplay, too.

While I grew up, my family circle grew up and out, too. When my brother joined us, life became a little more frantic since he was less an angel than a free spirit. Mother had to give him a" talking to" sometimes. I recall one incident when he was four years old. He ran up the back alley to avoid the irate words and Mother jumped on her bicycle and pedaled up the front to meet him at the corner. With that means of escape closed to him, John behaved like a little angel — for a while.

When John started to school, the children were planning to run him through a belt line for initiation to some club. Mother's bicycle became a handy tool once again. She jumped on that bike and pedaled over to the school to give the principal a piece of her mind. She told him that John had recently had an appendicitis operation and for that reason and plain good sense, she would not put up with allowing his classmates to whip him with belts. That was the end of the story: mothers can surely be fierce when their children are attacked.

John, also, was fun-loving but in a different way. Daddy used to say that things went into one ear of a person and out the other. So John would put his finger in his ear while Daddy was telling us something and when he finished John would take his finger out and say "Thar she blows. What did you say?"

John loved dogs and horses and he kept a horse at our local fairground when he was a teenager. He would wake early in the morning and deliver the local newspaper to earn pocket money, then feed his horse, and head for school. He had a small carriage for the horse to pull, and I recall one incident when he pulled up with his horse and carriage and a neighbor child said "Mommy, the garbage man is here!" In those early years, garbage was collected by men using horses and carriages. Cars and trucks were around then, too, and I recall one car with a rumble seat and running boards. I think it belonged to a relative of ours, and it made many laughs and smiles.

Horses were still pretty useful animals in those early years. When John was almost three years old, Mother looked out the window and saw him playing in the street with a horse dropping. "Put that down, John, it's horse manure," she said. John sniffed the item and said "Huh-uh! Poop!" Well, we couldn't argue with that test and assessment. He never used that "toy" again, or at least we never caught him.

Animals were part of our family circle and the larger community, too. We had several different dogs when we were children and one poor little thing, Pep, became paralyzed in his back legs. I used to take him with me to the nearby store in my wagon. If I didn't, he would try to follow me. In later years, I had a "hunting" dog named Mike - I was always hunting him. Vicki was our last dog. She used to lie under Mother's bed, and when people came to visit, Vicki would "sing", really howl, and scare some of them. Families can do that, too, when they contain lyrical canine members. We had other pets along the way; I had a bird and Daddy had a cat. He had a cat much longer than I had a bird! Circles can get eaten, it appears.

John used to visit Daddy's family on farmland some distance from home during vacations from school. He was about seven years old when he told Uncle Walter "I like your jackass better than Grandpa's horse-ass." Our family loved language and laughter. John enjoyed farming and in later years he and his wife, Marilyn, bought a house and some land 12 miles from town.

After World War II started in 1941, many things were rationed. Gasoline was one of them and this made it difficult for me to come home from school as often on weekends as I had before the war. For holidays, weekends and for the summer Daddy drove 32 miles both ways to bring me home for a little while. Mother and Daddy used their own ration shoe coupons for their growing children's footwear-needs.

Running Around In Family Circles with Friends in Pursuit

During the war we had Saturday classes so that the school years would be shorter and we would save resources. Other important things rationed were shoes, sugar, coffee and bread. The prisoners at the Ohio State Penitentiary baked bread for our school, and in later years I quipped that I had eaten prison bread. That lifted many an eyebrow, I am told. I hope it did, since that was my aim in saying it.

One day John took what he thought was a boiled egg out of the refrigerator and pointing to a spot on the floor he said, "Here is Tokyo and this is a bomb. Then he threw the egg on the floor, splattering everything with the raw egg. We used to have practice air raids and there were blackouts at night during the war years. The absence of light did not bother me as much as it did the others, of course, but I still noticed it. One night when I was about eight years old, Mother turned out the light in our bedroom and told my sister and me to go to sleep. In bed, I was reading a story to Bernie from a Braille book and I continued to read. The light was not necessary when I was reading Braille and Mother had forgotten!

People expanded the family circle. Bernie and Robert Baker were married in 1950 and Bob served in the Marine Corps. Soon after marriage the Marines were recalled for service in Korea and Bob was stationed at Camp Lejeune in N.C. After a few months Bernie went to live near the camp until Bob was discharged in August 1951. Later, Bob was employed as a mold-maker for Anchor Hocking Glass Corp. for 43 years. Bernie worked in the office there for some time, too, and when he was not at work, Bob has been wonderful to me over the years. He mows my grass, does household repairs, and even added siding to the house with no help at all. When an appliance such as the furnace needs repair, Bob comes over and watches the workmen like a hawk or my own eyes.

John served in the U.S. Navy for four years and he and his wife, Marilyn McLaughlin, lived in Norfolk during the first years of marriage. I visited them there and toured the USS Orion, which was John's home base ship. Like Bernie, John and his wife and their new baby, Kathy, returned to live 12 miles from here. John worked as a machinist for Anchor Hocking Glass for a number of years and then had a management job for another company until he retired.

Marilyn and John used to take me roller skating when we were in high school and John bought a pair of shoe skates for me so that I would have my own when the State School took us skating occasionally. One night when we were skating a child fell in front of Marilyn, causing her to fall, also. Then I managed to step on Marilyn. It was a big pileup but no one was hurt and I said "We will learn to do this right in a few more sittings."

After my college days, Marilyn and John took me bowling. We bowled several times a week and the owner of the bowling alley had a special rail made so I could hold onto it and throw the ball. When I managed to hit the pins, they sometimes fell in such a strange pattern that everyone laughed. This did not bother me at all. I joked about the "Spares and Strikes Forever March" and had a good time.

As we grew older, our sporting events grew tamer and tamer — going out to dinner together. We went out to one of our favorite restaurants just two days before John died.

When Daddy died, Mother went to work at the local hospital. She worked in the emergency room for a number of years and she would tell us about accidents and warn us to be careful. She worked in the nursery for a while back then, and after that in surgery. She continued work there for several years and then worked for local doctors. If Daddy and Mother had not worked so hard, I would not have a home today, for Mother, always wise, left the family home to me when she passed away in 1992, as a lifetime legacy. The other siblings had homes, so she left the family home to me to use as my home for as long as I need it. Then it will pass back to the other children.

When my hearing began to fail, Mother was wonderful helping me to develop a communication system. She was the last person I was able to understand. She printed capital letters in my hand to tell me about important events. Almost everyone can print, so I never expected others to learn a special communication system just to talk to me. After all, my hands are attached and I felt it was unnecessary to carry any other heavy equipment around for communication. Even the little children in our family still learn early how to talk to me in my hand, something they seem to enjoy and are proud to know.

After Mother retired from work at a doctor's office she worked part time for a local rest home until she was 72 years old. Then she had a few years to enjoy some trips with the Senior Citizens. One of these trips was to Hawaii and we have a scrapbook of pictures and other things from her trip there.

Mother passed away just six weeks before her 85th birthday. We still miss her. Mother's last words were "Take care of Georgia", and Bernie and others have diligently followed this final directive. For ten years every morning that Bernie is in town, she has come to assist with breakfast and other things such as reading bills. She has not been away from home more than a few days in any year and not every year. My aunt, Patty, does my heavy work and laundry and brings dinner several days each week. Years ago I did this all myself, but then my online work became so time-consuming I could not keep up with both jobs, and now a couple of mobility problems make it difficult to perform household chores. John's wife brings dinner to my home once a week. She used to come more often but she is semi-retired now and is in town only one day a week.

John passed away in 1994. He was working outside washing his antique car when he suffered a massive heart attack, like Daddy. It was just six weeks before his 61st birthday. After six years alone, Marilyn married Paul Tipton. We recognize the fact that it would be unfair to expect Paul to replace John, but he is a fine man and we all like him and watch the family circle wending its way. Bernie and I are the only ones left from the original family, but there are many offshoots from these roots.

CHAPTER 3

THE EXTENDED FAMILY:
My first circles multiply

William and Cynthia Griffith produced 11 children and at this writing one daughter is still living at almost 95 years old. She is in a rest home, however. This large family lived some 40 miles away so we did not see aunts and uncles often, but we visited various ones from time to time. I sometimes stayed a few days with Uncle Walter and his wife Mary and sometimes with Nancy and her Husband, Clarence. Our whole family traveled down to visit Daddy's younger brother, Art, and his wife occasionally for a Sunday trip. Art played a guitar and we called it a deetalee because he would tap his foot and sing, "Dee-ta-lee-a-lee-lee-lee."

The grandparents did not live close enough to us for us to have a wealth of memories, but Grandma did come to visit sometimes. On one memorable occasion at breakfast Mother asked if Grandma wanted more coffee. Grandma replied "Just enough to take the bad taste out of my mouth." We always giggled about that. After Grandma passed away, Grandpa came to visit us fairly often and my most vivid memory of him is sitting in a comfortable chair reading his newspaper.

My maternal great-grandmother, Mary, lived at our house the last year or so of her life. She had had a stroke and Mother took care of her. Mother used to say that if "Ma" had lived in our time she would not have died so soon. She had high blood pressure and medications for that are much improved now. I was away at school a lot of the time but when I was home I would come downstairs each morning and give "Ma" a kiss. She called me her little angel.

Grandma Moore's sister, Georgia Mae Horseman (Aunt Mae), and her husband (Uncle Mac), had no children and they liked to borrow us to take home with them. They lived in Shadyside, in southern Ohio. We would arrive during summer vacation from school and from there Aunt Mae would take us to see Washington, DC and the surrounding states. While we were in DC, we often visited a Hilary family and John Hilary let me drive his car — at least I shifted gears for him. He took us to see things like the tomb of the unknown soldier, the Washington Monument, and other famous places. When Uncle Mac and John's wife, Florence both passed away, John and Aunt Mae married and moved to a house not far from ours. John had retired by then but Aunt Mae continued her sewing hobby. Aunt Mae was a seamstress and she did a lot of sewing for us, altering garments, hemming up skirts, etc. I recall Fourth of July celebrations we watched from one of Aunt Mae's upstairs windows.

Beatrice and Russell Moore produced five children and, again, only one is still living. Mother's baby sister, Patty, has been a tremendous help to me since Mother's death.

Family circles make for coincidences that renew and enlarge home feelings. I was born on my Aunt Alma's birthday and we always had a special bond between us. Aunt Alma and Uncle Raymond (Grandpa Moore's brother) had no children of their own and they enjoyed having our family visit them. Aunt Alma helped with sewing my clothes for school and in other ways whenever she could. When I was small I called her Aunt Audi and that name stuck with her the rest of her life.

Grandma Moore lived to the age of 89, and Grandpa was 84 when he left us. Grandpa worked in a shoe shop for many years at the Boys' Industrial School, an alternative education facility here. He loved to plant garden vegetables, raise chickens and ducks, and he carried on our garden for a long time after Daddy's death. I used to cook dinner for Grandpa when he was working outside.

When Mother was two years old, my Grandpa had some baby ducks. Mother was playing with the babies, holding them under water and saying "Fim, duckie, fim." Of course, she was lovingly drowning them, but luckily Grandpa caught her quickly. Later, Mother learned to drive a car at age 13 and she said her dad always let her have the car while he rode his bike. Grandpa loved the county fairs and animals, and after the duckie episode, so did Mother.

Grandma was an example of that age's use of child labor, having gone to work in a shoe factory at the age of 13. Later on, Grandma did a great deal of cooking and preserving vegetables and fruit for winter, labor she said she loved. Most of her food was wonderful but she did make a few mistakes. I recall a party she had where she served homemade ice cream. She had forgotten to add the sugar but that did not prevent her from asking the guests if they wanted more. There was a lot of ice cream left over that day.

Another day Mother was bathing her sister Mary Margaret's little boys and teasing them about getting their tootsies wet. They started calling her "Toots" and she was Toots ever after. For many years, Mary Margaret and her husband, Albert, lived across the street from Grandma Moore. They had two sons, Gerald William (Butch), and Richard Alan (Dick). When Dick was a baby he threw his nursing bottle down one day and it broke. Butch said, "Just let him cry till payday." I think this was the first indication that four-year-old Butch might be interested in a career in business.

Albert built some houses, among other ventures. When we sold our first house and built a new one in 1964, Albert directed the building crew. For a time he also installed new carpets to earn a living. Toots' baby sister, Patty, married George Johnson in 1947 and I played the organ for the wedding. George served in Germany in the U.S. Army during the Korean War. I recall a trip to New York to take him to his ship to travel to Europe. On that occasion I saw the inside of The Statue of Liberty. We went home through New Jersey and I was intrigued by a sale on dresses there. All dresses marked $2.98 were, on that day, selling for $2.97!

Our family often went to a nearby lake region to swim and sail. Several times we rented a cottage at this area for a week or two of vacation. Patty and George, Marilyn and John, Toots and Daddy and others were part of the group. We also went to an area a little further away for a Sunday swim and picnic sometimes. This Lake Hope area seemed larger to me than the Buckeye Lake area. I never really learned to swim and I always claimed it was because I volunteered for the lifeguards and so I did not have to learn. I was included in a swimming class when I was five years old but I did not like having water dripping from all over me, although I enjoyed playing in the water so long as I kept my head out of it.

The circle is so varied. Patty and George owned a florist's business for many years. They still miss the flowers and travel around to see what other florists are doing. Patty and George have three adopted children. The oldest, Deborah, is a registered nurse working in a school for children with disabilities. She assists with feedings and functions that require medical knowledge. Chris is employed by a local restaurant chain and he likes working with food. Darrin works for a national bank in Columbus.

Toots had two younger brothers, but James Hannibal was 13 years older than Augustus Edward. In early days bread and milk were delivered at homes and Uncle Jimmy drove a milk truck. Sometimes, when we children were too rowdy, Toots would ask us what we would do if she went away. I said "Uncle Jimmy will bring us milk and Dana (a storekeeper nearby) will give us cereal." That was a four-year-old's idea of survival.

Uncle Jimmy used to sing in barbershop quartets and I recall several concerts I attended to hear him perform. He and his wife Helen (Babe) had two sons. The younger son, Thomas Lowell, is still living but the older one, Donald Lee, passed away about nine years ago. When Tommy was about two years old he had an ear infection and Toots would stop in to give him an antibiotic shot. For some time after that every time Tommy saw Toots, he would hide behind a chair and hold onto his bottom. One day when Tommy was six years old his mother saw him carrying a glass of water across the street to a neighbor's yard. In a little while he was back with another glass of water. She asked him what he was doing and he said "You know that bush in the preacher's yard? It's on fire and I am putting it out." More survival techniques for children.

Running Around In Family Circles with Friends in Pursuit

Toots' younger brother, Augustus Edward (Gus or Ed), was one of the most fun-loving people I have ever known. One day, Daddy and John were planting the garden and Ed came up behind them with a handful of seeds and said, "Here, you dropped these."

Ed and Jayne Ricker from Chicago had three sons, Wayne Edward, Timothy James and Marty Joe. Jayne's best friend passed away in Chicago before Marty was born and Jayne vowed to name her next child after that friend, Marty Jo or Marty Joe. The friend was a woman and the child was male, but he is a memorial to that close friend. Words allow memories to survive.

Wayne died in a motorcycle accident 12 years ago. I remember Wayne as a cute but sometimes ornery little boy. One day he was tearing up a loaf of bread and throwing it outside. His mother asked what he thought he was doing. Said Wayne, "I'm feeding the stool pigeons." Tim always claimed that his mother had to tie a pork chop around his neck to make the dog play with him. Obviously, Tim inherited some of the family's love of fun.

Whenever Uncle Ed told his family about accidents that the emergency squad had to handle, Tim always wanted to know what kind of car had the accident. That seemed to be very important to him, although the people were, too. Below are some interesting comments about Uncle Jim and Uncle Ed from Ed's son, Tim.

"Dad quit high school and joined the Civilian Conservation Corps in the early 1940s. I saw a park in West Virginia he helped build. He went from there to the Navy for the duration of World War II. He served on a destroyer named USS Fayette in the Pacific as a Boatswain's mate. His job was to take soldiers and supplies to shore in a water craft called an LCVP (Landing Craft Vehicle Personnel). He said he felt sorry for the soldiers that he dropped off because when they let the front to the LCVP down a lot of them didn't make it all the way ashore. After Dad's service in the Navy he became a firefighter here.

"Uncle Jim died in 1967 at 54 years of age. Ironically, Dad was on call at the firehouse that night. Dad said when he got back to the firehouse, all of the other firefighters had gotten up, made coffee, and waited for his return. I remember Dad and I had some horses to deliver the next day. I asked him if he wanted to take the day off. He said no, he would rather keep busy.

"Dad died on May 10th 1981. It was mother's day and he had been on duty at engine house the night before. The morning he died, he rode his motorcycle home, parked it in the garage and changed out of his work clothes. Mom got up a couple hours later and found him dead on the couch with the Sunday paper.

"The night before Dad died, Kathy (Tim's wife) and I went down to take Mom a gift for Mother's Day because we had plans on Sunday. While Kathy and Sarah (their daughter) visited mom, I slipped over to have a cup of coffee at the firehouse. Later, after I left, Wayne, Marty and Wayne's son Darin came to the firehouse. They shot pool and ate pizza. About 3:00 in the morning, Art Bevinger (another firefighter) saw Dad sitting in the firehouse kitchen, in the dark, with a puzzled look on his face. Art asked Dad what was wrong. Dad told Art, 'All of my boys came to see me tonight. They have never all showed up here on the same night. Something is wrong.'

"On the day of dad's funeral (May 13, 1981), someone shot the Pope. It was a very surreal day."

When I attended the State School for the Blind, we were promoted from the eighth grade in a manner similar to high school in today's world and we had a program. My eighth grade graduation focused on the Armed Services, since we were near the end of World War II. We sang all the theme songs of the various services and at that time, the women's auxiliary groups had special songs, too. These songs reflected society's feelings at that time in history. Often a women's song could be sung at the same time as the main theme and produce interesting counterpoint and harmony. The song for the WAVES, (Women Accepted for Volunteer Emergency Service), for example, fit nicely with "Anchors Aweigh" the Navy theme. Perhaps I remember this combination more vividly because Uncle Ed was the only family member who fought in World War II and he served in the Navy. Uncle Ed was wounded in WWII but it was not by enemy fire. His leg was broken when he caught it in an anchor chain, and he had a metal plate in that leg for the rest of his life. Aunt Jayne passed away in 2000 at the age of 72.

The WAVES sang:

Running Around In Family Circles with Friends in Pursuit

WAVES of the Navy there's a ship sailing down the bay
And she won't slip into port again until that vict'ry day.
Carry on for that gallant ship and for every hero brave
Who will find ashore his mansized chore
Was done by a Navy WAVE.

As might be expected, my family circle is still growing. Bernie and Bob and Marilyn are great-grandparents now and I am a great-great-aunt (pardon the bragging.)

Avery Christopher, our youngest family member.

CHAPTER 4

My Sister's Children: New family circles

❧

Bruce

We lived close to my sister's house when the children were small, and I was often treated to funny observations from a child's viewpoint. Bernie and Bob have four children, all of whom are successful in their chosen fields.

Bruce is the oldest offspring and, although I was in college the first two years of his life, I was kept informed of his pronouncements. One day when he was just learning to talk, he came with his grandma to visit me and he saw a squirrel eating an apple. "Kidddley iddley awple, show Mommy," he intoned. His grandma explained that they could not catch the squirrel to show his Mommy.

Church has always been a part of our lives and many of my pleasant memories involve some part of religion. When Bruce was five years old he was singing in the children's cherub choir for a Christmas celebration. "Away in a manger no crib for a bed." Bruce waved at his grandma in the congregation and said "Grandma, I have to go potty." His grandmother took him downstairs and he said "When we go back may I sit with you?" "We're not going back", said Grandma. "Everyone knows what you went to do!" With a surprised look Bruce said, "Well, don't they?"

Bruce liked to play Sunday School with his friends and one day his mother heard him say "I'll be the Father, Mark (his younger brother) can be the Son, and Cheryl (a neighbor) can be the Holy Ghost." "What about me?" asked another neighbor child. "You can be 'Amen'" he was told.

When Bruce was three years old I had a lady from China visiting me for a month. One day we heard him outside telling the neighbor children "Come in and see the Chinese girl. She won't hurt you." He got out some of his toys to show Lucy and his Mother laughed because the toys plainly stated "Made in Hong Kong."

As children have a way of doing, Bruce soon reached the age when he needed to start kindergarten. He came home from class one time and yelled "Hurry up and open the door, Mommy. I have a surprise for you." His mother let him in and said "What's the surprise?' With a smile on his face, the little fellow stated "I lost one of my gloves."

When he was a little older his cat died, and he was burying it. His mother looked out the window and saw him sprinkling her good perfume on the grave he had made. She asked what he thought he was doing and he said "This is Holy water." He had seen ceremonies on TV.

In another incident Bernie was doing laundry in the basement and the doorbell rang. She rushed upstairs to see who had arrived but there was no one around. "Bruce, did you see who that was?" she asked. "That was me," said the little one. "I got lonesome and I knew you would come up to see who came."

After Bruce finished dental college he went into the Army and served in Germany for several years. He liked the people and decided to stay longer. He made many friends there and they still visit each other from time to time. When Bruce returned to America he and Carol Kearny married. When I first saw Carol she was a baby. Her mother, Barbara, attended Capital University at the same time I did and brought the baby to a meeting. Carol was playing with a bead necklace and I teased about her having a rosary. Capital is a Lutheran school and people at the meeting thought that was funny. Barbara was an excellent pianist and teacher. When her husband passed away she moved to Indiana so she could acquire her Master's degree and I lost track of the family until Carol and

Bruce started dating. What a coincidence, another circle!

Today, Bruce Baker, D.D.S., has been in practice for 20 years and is a high-tech, high-quality dentist. He is certainly not lonesome. Two daughters have joined this couple. Brooke is married now and Kathleen, a teenager, is happy in her surroundings. When Kathleen first started to Sunday School the teacher asked what to call her for short meaning Kay, Kathy, etc. "Just call me Ruth," the child declared.

Mark

Mark Steven joined the family in 1954. He was one of the funniest little boys we have ever known and we all enjoyed his antics. When Mark was a baby he wanted me to hold him whenever I was at their house. Toots said he probably thought I looked enough like his mommy that I'd do whenever she was busy in another room.

Mark used to wake early in the morning, stand up in his crib and proclaim "Turn on the TV; there's something good on television." There was nothing at all on TV at that hour but luckily his mother had always been an early riser. There was an extension of the phone in Mark's room and Bernie would hear him pick up the phone and say "I wanna talk to Grandma." When Mark learned to dial the time feature, one Christmas Eve he dialed time every few minutes all night and announced the time. Bernie bought our mother new nurse's shoes one year for Christmas and had them wrapped beautifully. As the first gifts were opened Mark took the paper off of Toots' package and said "Here's your shoes, Grandma."

Mark's speech improved with age, but when he was very small, the neighborhood children were calling him "Mawkie." Their dad said his name was "Mark" but the kids said "He told us himself his name is Mawkie."

Mark never did finish a story he started to tell us one day. "One day, tomorrow," he said, and when Toots laughed because Mark had such a funny expression on his face, Mark did not continue. When our little boy went to a doctor's office for a routine checkup the doctor asked him if he had any problems with his nose and ears. Mark replied, "Well, they get in my way when I put on my shirt or take it off." I am sure that can be a problem sometimes. Children like Mark take survival seriously.

Mark married Robin Williams and I played the organ for their wedding. They lived near us until after their son and daughter, Eric and Erin, were born and then they moved to a town about two hours drive from here. We missed them very much and when Mark found a job here they moved back.

Eric is finishing a tour of duty with the US Army and Erin is working and hoping to finish college sometime. Mark graduated from Ohio University with a degree in Business Administration. He has worked in a dairy for many years and is now a planner/scheduler for a large grocery chain.

Carolyn

Carolyn Ann was born in 1957 and since she was the only girl in the family we did our best to spoil her. She was a sweet little girl and very pretty. When she was two years old she used to look out the window each night at bedtime and say, "Night, Mare." The neighbor's name was Mary.

Children say and do funny things and keep us laughing, but usually they do not remember these pranks. When Carolyn was two years old she went into the bathroom, took hold of the paper and dragged it all over the house. I used to babysit for Bernie when she went to a meeting or a church event. I enjoyed all of the children but I was away more when the first two were small.

One year at Christmas time Carolyn went shopping with Toots. Secrets were something not too familiar to the three-year-old and Carolyn said "Let me show you where my mommy got your rope." Toots knew she was getting a new robe for Christmas. When Carolyn was just a little older she was again shopping with Toots and Toots was busy talking with a clerk about a purchase. Along came Carolyn with a handful of tags and said "Here." She had removed all the tags from the coats. The clerk was shocked and said "Oh, no!"

Carolyn was very pretty and when she was six years old she was dressed up for a party. Bernie said "You look so pretty let's go down to the church and let the pastor marry you." Carolyn replied, "Oh,

Mommy, he's too old!"

I recall a children's record Carolyn used to play. The French was a bit too much for a little girl and "Aloysius, gentil Aloysius. Aloysius, gentil plus moret," was reproduced like this: all the witches all the witches. All the witches out for Hallowe'en." Poor Alouette got Americanized.

After Carolyn married she did early computer work for the Bureau of Motor Vehicles for the State of Ohio until her first daughter was born and later she became office manager for her brother Bruce's dentist office. Carolyn, her husband Edward Readman (Griz) had two daughters, Heather (in nurse's training), and Jessica (still in high school). Both of these young ladies have been very friendly and helpful over the years and we have photos of them telling me secrets in my hand when they were toddlers. Of course, they were secrets from me, too.

Scott

Scott Robert joined the family in 1960. I saw him when he was only one day old which was unusual for the time but they let me hold the tiny baby for a short time. As he grew, Scott liked animals and at one time he thought he might be a veterinarian but he decided he liked to heal humans rather than animals and he became a family doctor.

Like the other children, Scott liked to visit with Toots and me and he told his dad it was quiet here. I used to ask him when he was here how many were at church and he always said "There were two there." I never discovered what he was counting, maybe teachers or boys in his class, but there were always two. Toots told him to say "There were lots of people at church."

I used to make homemade pizza for the whole family and Scott loved it. I recall a time when Scott went to a school sports event where they sold what they called homemade pizza and Scott told them "It's not as good as my Aunt Georgia's." There was probably no problem with misplaced ingredients, apples instead of peaches, and no sugar for anyone to forget, so he may have been correct. I hope so.

Scott Baker, M.D. married Renee Wagner, M.D. who is an anesthesiologist. The couple began their practices in a small town about an hour's drive from here but after their two children, Alexander Scott, and Madison Renee were born, the couple moved back here. For several years, Scott was head of a medical practice here and Renee worked at the hospital. In January, 2002, Scott set up his own practice but Renee is still working at the hospital. The interesting thing about Scott's practice is that he purchased a one-room schoolhouse, added patient rooms and set up practice there. The original land grant for the area where this property is located was signed by Thomas Jefferson so I feel that we are taking part in the making or continuing of a circle of history.

The children enjoy music and some people say that Alex has inherited some of my musical feelings. He is only 8 years old and Madison is 7 years old but they study music at Capital University. Music and words circle throughout family history.

Our budding pianists Alex and Madison Baker.

CHAPTER 5

My Brother's Children: a second sibling's circle

~~

Marilyn and John had three children and the youngest used to pray for a miracle so that her mother could have another baby - she wanted a baby sister or brother. Here they are, in brief:

Kathy

Kathryn Marie was born in Norfolk, Virginia in 1955, when John was stationed there in the Navy. We did not see these children as often as Bernie's because when they moved back to Ohio they were still 12 miles away. Kathy became accustomed to attending a Catholic church with her Mother. One year to celebrate Mother's day the whole family went to church with Toots and when the ushers passed around Communion Kathy said "No, thank you, I ate at home." Wasn't she a polite little girl? We needed such a wit in the newest generation, to uphold our family's traditions.

John had horses at his place and I would sometimes go out to ride the horses with Kathy. Actually, I was surprised by feeling the horse under me. I did not think that something so stuffed with hay could be such a hard seat.

Kathy remembers watching me learn to bowl. The owner of the bowling alley, Ernie, would point to the ball and say "Look, Georgia, you did it" when I hit the pins and he knew I could not see his action. He would wiggle his hand at the ball to help it go to the pins instead of the gutter. Kathy said her dad just sat and smiled from ear to ear. When she was about 5 years old, Kathy said she listened to me playing the piano and wished it would sound like that when she played it. She seems to have been amazed at things I just took for granted and that I simply went ahead and did. It is warming to have such admiring relatives. Warm parents, warm children, warm grandchildren—that is a great recipe.

Kathy has three sons, all of whom are grown, and two of them have children of their own, making her a young grandmother. When John passed away Kathy said Ohio would never be the same without him but she lives in Michigan now.

John Carl

John Carl was born in 1958 and, like me, he was very musical. He graduated from Capital University, also, and he still sings a great deal. When John Carl was 5 years old he liked to watch the bigger kids ride their bikes down the hill in front of the house. He wasn't riding a 2-wheeler yet, but he didn't let that stop him! He pushed his tricycle up the hill and then hopped on for the ride of his life! His feet couldn't keep up with the pedals, so he quickly lost control. The tricycle flipped and he slid (face first) down the hill, which of course was gravel. Marilyn picked the gravel out of his forehead and then put mercurochrome on it. Kathy, who was 8, called me Dr. Frankenstein, which made John, well......!

John Carl used to call sour kraut "pickles" when he was young and he heartily disliked the smell. Marilyn would make kraut in a big crock in the basement and every time she would stir it and then can it, John would get one of his Dad's big red handkerchiefs and wrap this around his face and nose, bandito-style. The trick was, he would put some of Dad's after-shave lotion on it, trying to cover the kraut smell! Now, years later, John's the General Manager at Schmidt's in German Village! They sell hundreds of pounds of kraut a day, and John Carl had better not call them "pickles".

When John was 16, and driving he had his own car, which amazed me. It was a 1956 Studebaker. Kathy, now 18, had a habit of being late getting home. They kept a house key 'hidden' in the

Running Around In Family Circles with Friends in Pursuit

garage so they could get in without waking their mom and Dad. Dad told them that the next time they were late, he would take the key ... and they'd better not wake him trying to get in! So, you guessed it ... John was late! He looked for the hidden key and sure enough ... it was gone! So, thinking his Dad had taken the key, he stretched out in Mom's car to sleep. Around 5:30 am, his Mom opened the garage door to empty the coffee grounds, and ..wow. Naturally, and loudly, she screamed "What the devil are you doing in the Garage?", she asked. John told her that he was late and Dad had taken the key, so he had played it safe and slept in the car! She asked him why he hadn't tapped on the bedroom window, and he asked her if she was out of her mind: Dad had told them not to wake him!

Marilyn did some checking and found the key in Kathy's room, of all places It seems she came home before John and, thinking he was home already, didn't put the key back. She was "grounded", while Mom, Dad and John had a good laugh. She did later, too.

John Carl Griffith married Shelly McPherson and they have twin sons and one daughter. The twins like computers and while one, Cameron, plays trumpet, his twin Dane plays football. Their sister Megan studies art at 9 years old.

Susan

Susan Elaine was born in 1965 and she was a tiny baby. I used to crochet booties for the babies but on Susan they looked like snowshoes. Susan was fun and sweet. I recall one day when she was scribbling with a pencil and paper. She took the paper to her mother and said "Keep this until I learn to read." Smart four-year-old to preserve her writings. On another occasion when Susan was 4 years old, her mother was working and Kathy and John were supposedly babysitting with her. Kathy had been assigned to do the laundry and she tried to delegate the job to Susan, who was much too small to handle taking clothes out of the washer and putting them in the basket. Kathy and John put the little girl into a clothes basket and shoved the basket down the basement stairs. What a strange ride that must have seemed!

Big brother learned the hard way not to pick on this little girl. He used to try to make Susan get off the sofa so he could have t hat place. He would put a pillow over her head and punch the pillow. Susan had had enough of this so she left the sofa and John lay down. She put a pillow over his head and raised her fist. At the crucial instant John removed the pillow and Susan hit him squarely in the nose. After dealing with this nosebleed John never pulled the pillow stunt again.

Susan has a loving memory of one of her dad's antics. In high school she was in the flag corps. She used to take her flag out side and practice frequently because she loved being in the corps. One day her dad stood behind her with a broom and imitated her actions and everyone started laughing. At that time she did not think this was so funny and she cried, but now she realizes they were laughing at her dad, not his model.

Susan and Thad Goodman have two daughters, Kaylan is 13 years old and plays basketball; in fact she just attended a ball camp at Capital University. She loves to read and is a talented singer, having solo parts in her church. She plays flute and clarinet and as an 8th grader this year she can hardly wait to join the high school marching band. Music is a family love, just as fun with language is.

So is teaching, I think. Kaylan hopes to be a professional singer and teacher. She is well on her way to that goal. Gabrielle is 11 years old and she loves animals. She has 5 cats and her own dog, a toy fox terrier that weighed only 2 pounds at six weeks of age. The dog, Annie, weighs four pounds now and will grow to about 6 or 7 pounds. Gabrielle wants to be a veterinarian or vet's assistant. We wish her luck! Thad sells drywall products and Susan works part time in the office of the school her children attend.

CHAPTER 6

New Families: Finding Technology Circles

∽

Early in the 1970's a new device, the Optacon (OPtical to TActile CONverter), was invented. With this device a blind person could feel the shape of a print letter one letter at a time which vibrated. Since there was no limit to the size of a symbol that could be felt the device was useful for many things. I borrowed on my life insurance so I could purchase one of these machines. A good friend of mine who wrote beautiful cursive script wrote the training manual out in cursive and I practiced on that. I had learned the shapes of music notes and symbols through raised drawings while I was in school so I also practiced on those symbols and found the Optacon very useful. There were times when I needed sighted help because the music text was too cluttered with signs to distinguish all of them but Toots had learned to read music when she was a child so help was always available.

When I joined CompuServe in 1981 I was rather frightened of the big Monster On-line. I almost thought, as many new members do, that someone was watching me. My feelings in these early days have helped me deal with mistakes made by new members, like the lady who was sure Sysops sat in little booths and listened to everything they said. When I tell new people about some of the silly mistakes I made they begin to relax and enjoy themselves.

I always thought a cursor was someone who swore and logging was what was done to trees. In those early days the system would say "Enter blank line to continue," and I would laboriously type 80 blank spaces and press CR. Later I learned that all I had to do was press CR. When we told the system to "go" somewhere, for which we now can use a keyword, it would reply "Request recorded, one moment please," and that polite notice added to the feeling that someone was watching. Friends re-assured me that it was only a machine. At a dinner given by CompuServe in that early period a pastor gave a blessing and a voice came over the speaker "Request recorded, one moment please." Sometimes the system talked to itself when a member transferred from one host machine to another. I think the funniest message we ever saw was "Garbled yo-yo data," meaning that the first host had sent a message the second could not read.

After a few sessions on-line I was contacted by another member who was using the same type of equipment I was using, the classic VersaBraille. We exchanged a few E-mails and then decided to get together in the conference area. Howard Goldstein has been a tremendous help for over 20 years in dealing with problems of communicating with Braille devices.

The first VersaBraille machines were either smart terminals or dumb computers. When they were attached to a computer to use as a terminal, they could use only programs that worked through DOS (Disk Operating System). They were not DOS-based machines themselves but as a terminal with a computer they were limited to programs that used DOS. The VersaBraille could not download files but it could capture in text. One feature of this early machine was a real help but was not continued in later devices. These machines, as well as more modern ones, have only one line available, although the line length has grown.

The classic VersaBraille had only 20 columns on that one line, but the display did not scroll and leave us with nothing but the cursor to read as later machines do. What was on the display stayed there until the reader was ready for more text. I still use a classic VersaBraille for face to face communication. A good friend of mine developed a keyboard attachment that can be used by a second person to type to me. The keyboard is an early model of a computer keyboard and any typist can use it.

In late 1981 I became a section leader for "Handicapped Issues" and we held weekly conferences. Howard was one of the main participants and later his brother, David, joined us. We held these conferences for a few years and then Howard and I continued to meet to discuss life in general for an hour almost every week. I recall one session when Howard was explaining the difference between a bug and a glitch. Without thinking about it too carefully, I asked "Howard, do you mean that a bug is the son of a glitch?"

When the forum owners left CompuServe in 1982, I inherited the managing Sysop's job. This forum, then called a SIG (Special Interest Group), was for the general public, not just people with disabilities. I worked hard to make the forum a paying service and for some time it was one of the most popular forums. Many people felt it was a sad day when the forum closed in March, 2000 and merged with another of my forums, Political Debate.

In 1984 I purchased my first real computer and used the VersaBraille as a terminal with that machine. I had early speech screen readers that could be used with Braille devices but access was still very limited. One of the CompuServe programmers taught me a great deal about programming and this has been a good background for understanding software. He helped me configure the early computer and I am grateful for his training.

Some people think I have a dedicated Braille computer, and these are available, though mostly in Europe, but I prefer to use an off-the-shelf computer and attach a Braille display. This method of access is necessary for people who are employed in regular offices and must use the same machines other employees are using.

In 1984 I received an E-mail from a man named Chuck Lynd. Chuck asked if I would be willing to serve on an advisory board for the government-funded Council for Exceptional Children. I agreed to do this and the board functioned for three years. At that time Chuck worked for a company called LINC Resources and they asked me to join them to manage the IBM Special Needs Forum This forum was sponsored by IBM for four years and when they left CompuServe I continued the forum for another ten years and by then the web provided many options, making the forum unnecessary.

When the government contract that funded LINC went to another company, LINC disbanded and Chuck went off to work for Ohio State University. Over the years Chuck and his family have become very good friends. Chuck's sister, Connie, helped me purchase a second VersaBraille machine for a backup and she also helped with expenses such as service agreements. Special equipment is very expensive and maintenance is high-priced. The first VersaBraille machines were priced at five thousand dollars, and then they went to six thousand for a while. These machines are no longer manufactured, but I still own and use a 20-year-old one for face-to-face conversations.

Connie also purchased a scanner for me. The early scanners were speech-based but the speech could be redirected to a Braille device. However, setting up a device like this can be difficult if you cannot hear any of the speech. Toots helped with this setup but when she was no longer here and Braille scanners became available, Connie again helped me acquire a Braille model.

When the first real Braille screen readers were released another good friend, Molly Glendenning, purchased one for me and at the same time I acquired an IBM PS/2 computer.

By 1992, I began to earn enough money to handle my own equipment expenses. I am grateful to the good friends who gave me a start in my technology field and have tried to pass on some of this help to others.

I now have eight computers but one is an old XT. Have you ever tried to get a computer-lover to dispose of an old computer? Like an old shoe, the old pc just seems so comfortable and familiar. But in tech circles, it seems so old. My newest computer is a five-month old set running the Microsoft XP system.

Keeping up with the seeing world on the web with the limited equipment available to the Braille-reading blind is a real challenge. Most of you can see the whole computer screen at one glance. We have only one line available to us and most of us use a forty column display. Eighty column displays are available but the cost is very high. The last price I heard quoted was $15,000 and since the forty column version could be purchased for $4,000 it seemed to me more sensible to have two forties, instead. Then I have a backup in case one machine needs repair. The classic VersaBraille machines had twenty column lines so these newer machines are a considerable improvement.

There have been experiments with full screen displays, but the problems involved have not been solved. One big problem is cost. One Braille cell, six dots, can cost a hundred dollars to produce and one screen would have at least 1,000 cells. This high cost of producing a Braille cell is one reason no one has tried to produce a digital Braille watch. The cost would be high, the watches would be much too large and heavy, and Braille cells could never be powered with a watch battery.

Another problem is the scrolling while writing Braille. Our fingers can read only two lines at most at any time and only three or four characters simultaneously.

Graphics can be another headache. We can turn them off completely, or turn off just certain types, but often a web site's output involves graphics even to receive information in text. When our machines encounter a graphics symbol which has no label the machine will display "graphic 283" or some other number. This number is generated by the CRC. A CRC, cyclic redundancy count, is a number generated by running some special formula over all the bits of a file. Any different combination of bits will give a different CRC number. A CRC is really just a more complex and accurate checksum.

CRC's are generally used to determine whether a copy of a file is the same as the original in situations where actually comparing the two files would be impossible. For example, when you transfer a file from one machine to another using a protocol like ZMODEM, a CRC is computed for each packet of data before it is sent. After the packet has been received, the CRC is computed on the receiving end. If the two numbers are the same, it can be assumed that the packet arrived without error. This display of numbers can be disabled as can many of the other features.

As you can imagine, there are times when we simply cannot find the icon we are hunting. I have some wonderful helpers in the on-line community. They will experiment with a program to see how many times it is necessary to press the tab key to reach a hidden icon or how many times to press the right arrow.

Tom Sims, a pastor from Fresno, California, taught me how to use the first version of CIM (CompuServe Information Manager), DOSCIM. When WINCIM was added, a tech support person, Fred Nadel, also from California, helped me continue learning about the software. Fred has continued to help me up to the present time.

Another helper is my webmaster, Dorr Altizer, who is an expert at finding things on the web and helping with new programs. Carol Roper helps to research items and Chuck Lynd continues to assist in any way he can. All of these people will be introduced in more detail in later chapters.

My friends say I always have to be on "the bleeding edge" of technology and personal testing, and they are right. I love challenges and solving new problems. Life itself is a challenge and we all need to meet that challenge head-on! When new programs or operating systems are introduced I want to try them and I want to do the work myself. In early days when I purchased a new machine, Chuck Lynd would stop by and set it up for me, but Bob has learned enough about computers that he can do the initial setup now. After that, I ask a lot of questions, and friends like Fred Nadel and Dorr Altizer find the answers if they don't already know them.

We occasionally run across someone who is totally confounded by the notion of a blind person on the Internet. They ask "How can a blind person read a web site?" A person who is blind can use speech synthesis to navigate and communicate. Speech is cheaper but I think it is slower and less rewarding. It is much better, in my opinion, to see how words are spelled. I often see words confused like "sight" and "site" and there are often deliberate misspellings to make the speech synthesizer pronounce words correctly. Spelling is bad enough today without misspelling purposely. Today's synthesizers can be adjusted much better than they once were. In one of my first access programs we really did have an "ass key" to make the robot pronounce ASCII correctly.

There are many web sites that are not properly set up and the answer to the person who wanted to know how the blind can read a web site would be "They can't see your site." But the government has passed new laws requiring web sites to follow established rules for site creation.

If you would like to see a totally modern, world-wide accessible web site visit www.ggtechservices.com on the internet.

Actually, some of the awards I have received are the result of my participation in technology. In 1987 the mayor of Lancaster declared January 11 "Georgia Griffith Day" and there was a large get-together of citizens. These wonderful people had collected enough money to purchase a Braille embosser for me. This was an automatic embosser that operated from commands on my computer. Now my music proofreading chores were made much easier. Instead of having to recopy a whole page of Braille because of one omitted character I could use disks provided by the transcriber and insert the character, then reemboss the page. For this special event I received a letter of congratulations from President Reagan. Friends from NBA (National Braille Association) came to the party and the LINC workers attended. Bettye Krolick even managed to attend from Colorado.

Senator Mike Dewind admires Georgia's Smithsonian medal.

In 1996 I received the "great Communicator" award from the Central Ohio speech and hearing center. Colin Powell was the keynote speaker at that event. Although he was not autographing books that day he did one for me and this picture was taken at that session.

In 1997 I received a Smithsonian medal, which was for my work with the Handicapped Users' Database which I started on CompuServe in 1984. This service is no longer available on CompuServe but many of the files can still be downloaded from my web site mentioned above. All of the major players in the disabilities field are linked to this site and especially new ventures in the field. For example, many people do not know that there is a Braille embosser that can emboss Braille graphics now. This is something new. It was developed in the last year and other new access tools are linked to the GGTech site.

Georgia with Colin Powell at a reception before the award luncheon.

CHAPTER 7

Old Friends, Lost and Found: tracing school circles

Over the years, like most of us, I have lost track of most of my school friends but I have kept in touch with a few and three years ago I received a Braille letter from a woman whose name I did not recognize. It turned out I knew this woman fifty years earlier but under a different name. She was now using her first name and she had married David Stevens. I knew both Imogene Swann and her sister Clementine in school but I had not heard anything from or about her since 1950. Now Sue Stevens had just acquired a new computer and wanted to communicate. Her first computer set up was a Braille TTY device which did not live up to its expectations and she soon had a real computer screen reader. Like me, she had lost most of her hearing and we had much to discuss. We started exchanging notes and have communicates almost daily since that time. I am happy that I have been able to assist Sue with some computer problems. She has gained a lot of confidence and whether you are "disabled", "impaired", or "challenged", having that helps in every way.

The thing I remember most vividly about Sue was when she was the star of a novelty number we played in the band, "Little Brown Jug Goes to Town." Sue played piccolo in the band and she would stand up to perform the solo part but before she had a chance to start, some other section jumped up and began to play. Sue stomped her foot and sat down angrily. This was repeated until every section had played the tune as a solo. Finally, at the very end we let Sue perform the solo part all alone, with no accompaniment at all. Sue was in the eighth grade and admits now that she loved to show off at that age. It was a fun time, as eighth grade ought to be.

Sue and David have two sighted sons, Grant and David. When Grant was in the third grade his class was studying the human eye and the little fellow thought it would be fun to take his dad's glass eyes to show the class. His dad had graduated to a plastic version, but when he learned what Grant had done he was very embarrassed.

Sue also suffered embarrassment at work one day. She had needed medical information so she could use correct spelling in transcribing records. She requested a copy of a book from a Braille library. It had raised drawings of the human body and one day she dropped the book. Everyone was giggling but no one would say why until Sue picked up the book. She found it had fallen open to the page showing male private parts.

Dave passed away two years ago and we tried to make things easier for Sue. She has adjusted well to the loss but no one really understands this sort of thing until it happens to her.

I have kept in touch with a woman near Columbus for over fifty years. Janice Evans Blatz. She and her husband Vernon, both of whom attended the School for the Blind at the same time I did, have kept me laughing about things their three children did as they were growing up. Raising three seeing children is not easy for anyone but it is much more difficult for two blind parents. It can be fun, too, of course. Janice's sons used to take her to the grocery on their tandem bicycle and one day one of them drove her through the carwash. He asked if she was wet enough and she said "No." So he just turned around and went right back through.

Janice served eggs for breakfast one morning when her little daughter said "Mommy, I wish you'd sat on these til they hatched; I like chicken better." Now it is grandchildren who keep us laughing. Julie caught her little daughter scrubbing out the john with Julie's toothbrush. Janice commented that it was probably not the first time, just the first capture.

Vern kept a garden and the neighbors got a laugh out of seeing him working in the dark or mowing the grass after sundown. He was a programmer and was on-line for several years and we wish Janice would join us in this medium. Vern died about three years ago but I still stay in touch with Janice through Braille letters.

When I attended Capital University there were 1000 students and I was the only blind one. I had readers to read my assignments and when I could find a student taking the same course who was willing to read their assignment aloud to me we joked about them being paid to study. The State paid tuition, readers and books but Daddy paid room and board.

When I was a junior, another blind lady joined us in the music course. There was one course, harmonic analysis, which involved so much blackboard work that the instructor taught Beatrice and me privately, using piano compositions to illustrate his points. I lost track of Beatrice over the years and none of my friends seems to know what happened to her.

When I was a senior another friend from the State School joined us. I remember Roland Hudson as an excellent organist and the degree he earned from Capital and later a master's degree from DePaul University in Chicago were both in organ performance. Rollie did some radio work for eight years and played the organ on a substitute basis for both the Cubs and White Sox baseball teams.

Rollie represented the Yamaha company as a concert artist in 47 of the 50 states and could be heard on tapes and at teachers' workshops until the travel became a problem. He was sometimes in three different time zones during the same week; a new job option was also opening up at this time.

Today, Rollie manages the 800 line for Yamaha piano division. He answers questions mainly about their digital pianos and how they are used with computers. Rollie commented on how fortunate we were to have had good teachers at the State School and also at college. In working with Rollie, you have just met an accomplished artist.

Howard and David Goldstein were mentioned with reference to technology but they have also become good friends. When David was five years old he and Howard were listening to a TV version of "the

Land of Oz" that had a character named "Mombi the Witch." Their father taped the program for them and when David and Howard were discussing the program later their mother misunderstood and thought they said "Mommy the Witch." No matter how often the boys explained that she misunderstood, she insists with a smile that they regularly referred to her as "wicked Witch' or "the witch."

She was very proud of this title because to her it meant she was succeeding at encouraging her sons to do things on their own. This is a very close-knit family and they have had a lot of fun with the witch story. On her 25th wedding anniversary, they gave their mother a silver-painted broom. Whenever their mother talks about writing a book with their family's stories in it David says he should collaborate - she can write it any way she wants it and he can write the truth.

Howard and I still chat now and then for an hour or so and keep up on happenings in our lives. David and I exchange E-mails and on his birthday this year I sent him "happy birthday" written in a minor key. We used to have on-line birthday parties for these young men and a lot of people enjoyed them. We all seem to be busier than we were 15 years ago, though, so we don't have as much time to arrange or attend on-line parties any more.

Up to this point in my story, the friends I have mentioned have all been either schoolmates from the School for the blind or sight-impaired friends from on-line. Now we will meet some of my many friends who have no physical disabilities.

When we were small children, our family had what was then called "a hired girl" to come in and keep us entertained so Toots could do her housework. This "girl," (babysitter) named Lucille Engle, was always grateful that Toots gave her a start in life and she was a fine playmate and John, who could not pronounce "Lucille" at that early age called her "Loosh." I think Loosh was about 17 years old when she joined us and tried to keep us out of trouble.

When Loosh was doing the washing, one day John's belt buckle was ruined by the washing machine. John cried and ran to Toots sobbing and said "Loosh broke my belt." Whenever I see Lucille these days I always think of that and my standard greeting is always "Loosh broke my belt!"

Running Around In Family Circles with Friends in Pursuit

Years later Loosh married James Leroy Glenn, a machinist at the Diamond Power company (We always called him Leroy) and moved to Newark, Ohio. They became the parents of two fine daughters, Janice and Christine.

It wasn't until years later when the Glenns moved back to Lancaster that the families touched each other again. Lucille took her daughters for skating lessons one Saturday and Bernie was at the skating rink. Bernie and Lucille had a wonderful time exchanging memories and they vowed to stay in touch.

Janice owns a beauty salon which is about a block from my house and we have patronized that business for many years. Janice keeps my hair looking nice. Her sister, Chris, teaches reading in Bremen, a county school system, and Leroy and Lucille are retired now. Leroy, or Jim, worked for the Diamond Power Company for 36-1/2 years.

The impressive thing about this family is that they always travel as a group. Mom, Dad, Janice and Chris have been to every state in the union and they slept in the open car on many of these trips. Two years ago they all visited the Holy Land and this spring they traveled by bus to Washington, DC.

Bernie and Mary Alyce Doran were friends when we were still in high school but Mary Alyce has become a close friend of mine, also. She attended Capital University 12 years before I did and when I was home for longer periods after graduation from college we had more time to get acquainted. Mary Alyce (or M A as we often call her), used to take me to speak to school children and other groups about Braille and the education system for persons with vision disabilities. Some of these sessions produced gems of childhood wisdom and all were fun. After I talked with one third grade class and demonstrated reading and writing Braille, I played the piano for the class. One little fellow said "My teacher can play the piano better than you can. She can play with just one hand."

After I finished talking with a fifth grade class a little girl said "Thank you, Miss Griffith, for wasting your time." The teacher promptly explained that the child should try to say "for giving your time." It seems that the circle of what the universities call childhood malapropisms goes on in the new generation. I call it fun.

After most of these sessions the children wrote letters to me to express their thanks. Some of these were real masterpieces.

One of these letters read "Dear Miss Griffith, How do you find your mouth when you eat?" I have never lost it, I am glad to say.

At this time I was teaching private music lessons at home and also at the Maywood Mission, a place that gave underprivileged children music lessons at a reduced rate. At home I taught flute, piano, clarinet, trumpet and trombone but the mission children studied only piano lessons. I recall one little girl who was having trouble understanding scales. She would say "school" instead of scale. I told her it was like the scales on a fish and she asked "Then the fish goes from C to C?" Whoops.

I have many friends from my church and one in particular, Maryland Belhorn, always joins Mary Alyce to visit for my birthday. Maryland makes beautiful cakes and always has one tucked away for my party. I recall having my Aunt Mary, Uncle Walter's wife, make a sweater set for Maryland's baby daughter and this must have been nearly forty years ago.

In the late 1960's, when I began to lose my hearing, I could no longer teach private lessons. My college freshman roommate's sister, Ruth Warner, invited me to come to visit her and meet her eight children. While I was there Ruth took me to various large city help places to see if anything more could be done for me. Some exercises helped my general well-being and we tried various kinds of hearing aids but none could reverse the nerve damage. I had learned the shapes of print letters while at the State school and Ruth and her children helped me learn cursive. If I did not understand the shape of a letter, one of the children would cut a large sample of the letter from cardboard. This training was very helpful for use with the Optacon.

Toots was working 12 hours a day at the hospital during this time but all family members hoped something could be done to restore my hearing. I finally decided that the only path was to accept the fact that my hearing was gone and I said "I must get on this horse and learn to ride." I could still hear some things into the 1980's but the sound-discrimination loss was worsening.

After I returned home, Ruth wrote to me daily in Braille to keep me informed of major events. Although there were news resources in Braille, producing in that format was very slow and sometimes it took several weeks to produce a news magazine. Ruth kept telling me I did not need a college degree to do housework and I should find something worthwhile to do. I enrolled in the Library of Congress Braille proofreading course to try to turn off her constant comments about wasting my life. It worked.

One of the staff members at NLS was very helpful in getting me started in this endeavour and we have remained friends ever since. When I was in Washington, DC for the Smithsonian award I invited Maxine Dorf to join my staff members for dinner and a great time was had by all. Over the years I had talked with Maxine at NBA meetings and we still keep in touch.

After I was certified in literary Braille, Ruth's sister Jeanne invited me to visit her in Washington, DC, and on that visit Jeanne took me to visit the National Library Service. The librarians said I was just what they were hunting - a proof reader with a music degree. They gave me some tests and then I was certified in music Braille proofreading.

One of the first people I met through the music transcription program was Bettye Krolick. Bettye is a sighted, professional musician and she was writing a dictionary of Braille music signs. She traveled here from Illinois one wintry day to have me translate a French music book. As her project progressed, we found other languages were necessary. I bought dictionaries in the languages I did not know well and set out to help all I could. Languages are easy for me because I see the similarities between them and when reading in Braille these similarities become even more prominent. Each language still has only six dots to form a letter and although there are Braille contractions in all languages, the letters are formed the same way unless they are accented letters. A person soon becomes accustomed to these accented letters. I had studied two years of Latin and two years of French in high school and after college I bought books from Europe to teach myself Russian. With this new music project I set out to learn other languages - among them German, Danish, Swedish, Polish, Spanish, Italian, Portuguese,

Dutch - and isolated phrases in other languages whenever that was needed in my work.

Whenever the dictionary project slowed down for one reason or another and someone mentioned "the dictionary" I would ask in innocence, "What dictionary?" We finally finished the project, however, and many blind musicians are happy owners of this work.

As Bettye explained in her tribute to me, she was instrumental in helping me acquire my first connection to CompuServe. We became good friends and often traveled to or from an NBA (National Braille Association), meeting. NBA is an organization of mostly sighted transcribers of Braille - literary, music, mathematics, and graphics. The organization holds workshops twice a year in a different location each time. A local Braille group sponsors each meeting and I met many of the transcribers all over the country.

I would sometimes go home with Bettye for a few days and sometimes we visited a few days before a meeting. We held music Braille workshops for sighted transcribers at these meetings. I served on the NBA Board of Directors for six years and continued to proofread Braille music until 1989 at which time my other duties became too heavy to continue proofreading. For years I was the only Braille music proofreader working but when I went on to other things, there were two others available. Now it seems that there is no one available to do this work.

At the NBA meetings I always tried to arrange to meet someone from CompuServe since the meetings were held in a different city/state each time, twice a year. I have met many of my staff members and others from CompuServe and I always tried to have these people join us for a meal or the banquet.

Bettye and I traveled together to meetings at NLS, too and to some other important sessions around the country, like the Helen Keller Centennial. Bettye always tried to find some sightseeing things that I could feel to increase my understanding of life and the world. Recently I asked a blind friend what kind of a face he had. He replied "It's just a face." That is how I used to feel about faces until Bettye took me to a museum and let me feel the different kinds of faces. At places like zoos Bettye always found animals that we were allowed to touch. I have many pleasant memories of these outings.

Chuck Lynd and the LINCers continue to visit occasionally and have a Chinese dinner with me. Chuck has continued to be a tremendous help in many ways. When CompuServe began having live Business Partner meetings Chuck accompanied me to the meetings and typed as my interpreter. Chuck was manager of the Education Forum and I helped him there as much as I could. In 1999 Chuck's job became more time-consuming with many trips around the country and he asked me if I would take over the Education Forum. I found some really good staff members who help me keep this service alive and Chuck is still available for consultation.

A long-time friend and helper, Chuck Lynd.

In 1991 a tech support man named Fred Nadel joined CompuServe. This man can do more than just read and quote the manuals. He has found many techniques and tricks to make seemingly inaccessible services and software available to me and we have become cyber friends. He tells me about his grandchildren and I share funny incidents involving my nieces and nephews.

The following friends are also staff members and some are sponsors. More details will be given about them in the chapter on staff.

Tom Sims, an ordained pastor, joined us when The White House Forum was set up and he became a Sysop there. He was also named my chief assistant in the White House and later in Religion. When The Christian Fellowship Forum was born, Tom was the logical choice for assistant there.

Tom and I have become good friends and have discussed a variety of topics over the years. I met Tom twice when I traveled to California for meetings.

One Sunday Tom said that everyone who came into his church laughed at his bulletin. He looked to see what was so funny and read this announcement: "The choir will practice Thursday at 7:00 pm. The emphasis will be on male parts." All the women assured him they would attend this one. Tom laughs at himself, doesn't get angry with others and is a really nice man. When a member tried to insult him by saying "I don't know if you have enough intelligence to understand my situation or not." Tom replied, "Well, I haven't had my IQ tested for a while but I will certainly try."

Although Tom and I are not members of the same faith, we enjoy discussing religious topics and finding the similarities rather than the differences between our church homes.

David H. Tucker has been with my forums since early days and has become a friend. Dave has two sons, one is a musician in Austin, Texas, and the other is an engineer for a computer company in Minneapolis. Dave experiences the best climates, Florida in the winter and northern states in the summer. I met Dave when he attended the presentation ceremony of my Smithsonian medal.

Bev Sykes, who has also been with me since early days, also attended the Smithsonian presentation and I had met her a few months earlier when I attended a meeting in California. Later when their daughter's music group performed in Ohio Bev and her husband Walt came to visit for two days. The next year the musical was in Ohio again and Bev's mother came with the couple to visit. The mother commented that Jeri played flute, clarinet and saxophone in the same number and with mock-concern, I said "She must have a big mouth."

Carol Everhart Roper has been with us for over a decade and I have asked her questions about a number of things for this book. Sometimes it is faster to ask someone who might know the answer rather than spend time researching. I asked Carol "How long does an elephant live?" and she replied "Until it dies." Then she told me the life span of an elephant is 70 years and I knew my memory of the elephant mentioned earlier was correct.

Henry Neufeld has become a friend and has been a member for almost a decade. He became a sponsor in 2000 and continues his mission in three of my forums.

Over the past decade Jacquie Koplen has assisted with religion forum in many ways and she has been a very good friend. She was a tremendous help during the last month Toots was with us and showed real compassion. She would call the hospital for daily bulletins about Toots' condition and put the information on-line where I could read it. These were the days before anyone in my family had connected to E-mail. Much appreciation goes to Jacquie.

Nate Lenow has been on my staff since early White House Forum days. He often writes articles for political publications and he has worked in state and local government projects.

Jon Dainty also assisted in the White House Forum and in religion forums. When CompuServe asked business partners to bring an assistant with them to our last meeting, Jon was chosen to accompany me. He was closest and he took a couple of days vacation to attend. We have discussed many interesting topics including church music and have a friendly relationship.

Patsy Haggerty has assisted in the Religion Forum for almost five years. Patsy said she always thought people said "for all intensive purposes" but realized one day that it was really "for all intents and purposes." This reminds me of a lady in New York who wanted to use some of the local jargon in a letter to her parents so she wrote that her apartment cost "a nominal egg." Later, she learned that what people were saying was that it cost "an arm and a leg."

Dorr Altizer has been my webmaster for over four years and after 25 years in the Air Force, he says "Don't call me 'sir'!" I try.

CHAPTER 8

Bits, Bytes, Politics, and Religion: circling online

∽

In the early days of discussion groups on CompuServe, the services were known as Special Interest Groups (SIG). The original name for the Issues Forum, the first one I managed, was Newspaper Information Providers' Special Interest Group and if you think we were teased about that acronym you are correct. When the group left the service we decided to keep the acronym but change the name. For some time it was know as National Issues and People Special Interest Group. When SIG became forum and CompuServe became more international we shortened the name to just Issues.

The early forums had only ten public sections and we tried many different topics. When a section grew to the point that it dominated the discussions that section was given a forum of its own. One of the first topics to go was religion. Other topics moved away until the forum became known as "The Womb of CompuServe." Travel, News, Literary, Human Sexuality and many other topics went to their own forums.

In those early days we spent many hours chatting with others on-line in the conference area. Over the years the newness of the medium wore off and more time was spent in board discussions. A member could reply to a board message at any time of day or night and then go on with their busy life. We held some important guest conferences associated with the Issues Forum but most members preferred reading a conference transcript rather than sitting still for an hour or so. These forums are all for the general public not just for persons with disabilities. We have had a few members with disabilities but most people do not give this information and for years many of my members were unaware of my handicaps. There is a forum for persons with disabilities but it is not my forum. When the Issues forum closed in March 2000, it was still a large and popular service.

In 1991 I was asked to manage the Campaign '92 forum which was just being set up. One of my assistants from Washington, DC, had direct contacts with some of the political figures and this helped to gather information. Major candidates had sections in the new forum and major parties also had sections. One of the main problems with this new service, and one we had to monitor closely, was that some members thought it was fun to impersonate the Presidential candidates. We developed tactics to control this fakery and the election proceeded.

After the election, we reorganized the forum into a Political Debate forum and major parties still retained their sections. At that same time I was asked to manage the new White House Forum. Our original purpose was to give the White House a place to store press releases on CompuServe. We held discussions about these press releases and about the Administration's plans for the country. President Clinton sent "thank you" letters to all current staff in those early days. As more and more information became available on the Internet the need for storing it in a forum became less productive. This White House Forum was also consolidated into Political Debate in March, 2000. To say it was crowded is a major understatement. Sometimes we had three topics which had all been in their own sections merged into one section.

In 1991, I was also asked if I would manage The Religion Forum. This seemed like some kind of homecoming because the group had started in my Issues forum. Again, religion grew and two forums were moved out to their own areas. The Religious Issues forum lived until 2000 and the Christian Fellowship Forum is still available.

Some very important conferences have been held in The Religion Forum among them sessions with authors Gerald May, Thom Hartmann and Jon Erickson-Tada. In addition, we have had guest leaders on the message boards. We set up a temporary section for the guests for a month or sometimes longer and they come in when their schedules permit to post messages and answer questions about their work.

Pacesetters Bible School has held a number of conferences with leading theological figures about important religious issues. Dr. Alden Thompson, Professor of Biblical Studies at Walla Walla College in College Place, WA, was online for one of these sessions to discuss his book "Who's Afraid of The Old Testament God." We also had an important conference concerning prophecy about "the last days". Dr. Richard Rice, Professor of Religion at Loma Linda University was online to discuss his book "The Openness of God".

Dr. Harvey Brown, author of "When God Strikes the Match" (and contributor to "Power, Holiness and Evangelism") held a conference about revival movements in the church on one memorable evening. It was one of the largest conferences ever held in The Religion Forum. Dr. Brown, a former chaplain and then a college administrator, is now President and founder of Impact Ministries, Inc., based in Wilmore, KY.

I must say that working with politics has made me more aware of what is happening in the world today, and that working with many different religions has made me more tolerant of the beliefs of others.

I also manage The Education Forum on CompuServe. This service has never been huge but since it competes with all the free government education services on the Internet, this is not surprising.

There are many fine educators who enjoy discussing major issues with each other and often students raise questions about their schools or issues that concern them. One such recent student question was "Is it too much to ask teachers to return homework?" Apparently in this student's school homework was graded but not returned. The teachers discuss such issues as plagiarism, ways of attracting and keeping new teachers, and methods for helping gifted children.

CHAPTER 9

My Fellow Workers: circles online and off

Under the current AOL business model, Sysops must seek sponsors or advertising to remain self-supporting. I have been fortunate in finding some sponsors, who are also staff members and friends. At present, I have seven sponsors and some sponsor more than one section.

When an individual, company, or group buys sponsorship of a section, they are free to administer that section as they wish as long as they stay within the general rules for the forum.

Pacesetters Bible School sponsors Christianity in the Religion Forum and Prayer in the Christian Fellowship Forum. Henry E. Neufeld is the founding director of Pacesetters Bible School. He has BA and MA degrees in Biblical Languages, and has done post masters work in Linguistics. Neufeld has started numerous small study groups, in which he emphasizes building a present living experience using scripture as a foundation. He is the co-author of When 3 to 8 Gather, a guide to using scripture effectively in small prayer groups. He is also the vice-president of the steering committee for United in Prayer for Pensacola, a city-wide prayer movement. He grew up as the son of Seventh-day Adventist missionaries, left the faith, then returned to the Lord in a United Methodist Church. This has led him to concentrate especially on experience that transcends barriers of doctrinal belief.

Henry is also the link to www.energion.com, which sponsors the Scholar's Corner in The Religion Forum and the We the People section in The Political Debate Forum. His wife manages the Catholic/Orthodox section in the Religion forum.

Tom Sims is pastor of Baptist Temple Church, "The Fellowship of Joy," in Fresno, California. Through the years he has been involved in community affairs, non-profit management, and education as a teacher and advisor. He is a singer, writer, and story teller, a husband, a father of two grown sons, and an avid computer user. Tom tells stories about a fictional town called Polecat Hollow. He is interested in people and was once or twice a door-to-door salesman having once sold a Kirby in a house with no carpet. He is also interested in ideas and how people express them. Tom received his Associate and Bachelor's degrees from Bluefield College, attended Virginia Tech, and received a Master of Divinity from Golden Gate Baptist Theological Seminary.

Tom sponsors the Fellowship of Joy section in The Christian Fellowship Forum and is my Chief Assistant for that forum and The Religion Forum.

Carol and Lee Roper are the sponsors of Free Thought and Science/Philosophy sections on the Religion forum, and Carol is a sysop and staff manager on the Debate forum. Carol joined RF (Religion Forum) in 1992 as Carol Everhart and soon became a section leader for Free Thought, growing the section from a quiet one to one of the big five sections on RF. She moved up to sysop a year or so later, while going through a divorce. In fact, she met Lee there - he'd joined the forum in 1996, and found a number of like-minded folks in FT (Free Thought), and settled in. He and Carol began corresponding and the romance developed, and they married in early 1997. The Ropers have a gathering at their home annually for some of the wonderful friends they've made on the forum, and people have traveled there from all over the US, Europe and Canada. Both are atheists, share interests in sciences and philosophies, and are ardent supporters of equal rights.

Patricia Olver was raised in a small rural town in Pennsylvania with very conservative values. She now live in Dallas, TX and still feels she is conservative, but many consider her a bleeding-heart liberal - so she says that probably makes her a libertarian. Patricia is a firm believer in continually learning, and not becoming attached to any ideology. Philosophically, she calls herself a Taoist-Wiccan (!), but has no belief in a deity. Patricia began posting on CompuServe forums in the early 90s, primarily in places where there are discussions about philosophy, society and how we interact. She sponsors a section on the Religion Forum because she wants to ensure a continuation of such discussion boards in a moderated atmosphere.

Patsy Haggerty joined the Religion forum in 1996, following her brother Michael and her good friend Carol. She'd been a sysop on the New Age Roundtable (Forum) on Genie for 2 yrs. before that, and her expertise in handling members showed right away. Willing and able, she joined the Religion Forum staff as a section leader on soon after becoming a member, then moved up to Sysop within a year or two. She became a sponsor in 2000. Patsy's goals in sponsoring a section are to encourage open and respectful discussion on very difficult topics. First as a member of the Peace Corps, and now as a chemist for the Navy, Patsy has traveled around the world, giving her ample opportunity to study of the world's religions, and is knowledgeable about many of them (both modern and ancient). She brings a wonderful sense of balance to her forum work. Her upbringing was Episcopalian, and she now describes herself as an agnostic (or occasionally as a "godless heathen"). She is currently section leader for Interfaith Dialog, Hot Topics, and the Jehovah's Witnesses sections.

Rich Pevey joined the Religion Forum in 1990, and right from the start, he found himself involved in controversial discussions. When sponsorships came available, Rich offered to sponsor the Limbo Section, where many of the more contentious threads tend to wind up. He really enjoys digging deeply into his subjects, and is fascinated by the many different ways people choose to argue volatile topics.

Although he was raised as a fundamentalist Christian, Rich is now most comfortable calling himself a non-theist or atheist. He is a humanist, and has helped organize humanist groups in his area.

Rich is convinced that the surest way to find the kernels of truth in online discussions is by challenging other posters to carefully consider their words, and to take the time to make sense and we hope, to express an integrated world view. Rich believes that the value of this exercise will help him and others strive to make a bit more sense each time they enter a new discussion, and make forum discussions more interesting and lively.

Staff members are unpaid volunteer forum members who enjoy discussing the topics covered by a forum. When I was managing seven forums I had 140 staff members but since three forums closed, the number is closer to 80 now. Some staffers help in several forums and they are certainly appreciated.

Below are biographies of some of the staffers who have been with my forums longest. A few newer members are mentioned, also, but not all are included in this sampling.

David Tucker began his theatrical career on the showboat "Golden Rod" on the St. Louis riverfront at the age of 10. After the inevitable pause when his voice changed, he continued as a stage manager at the Grand Burlesque, the St. Louis Municipal Opera, and shows on Broadway and on tour. As a director and actor he has been engaged in local and regional theaters in St. Louis, New York, and elsewhere, most recently in Clearwater, Florida.

Tucker has also served as the Director of Performing Arts for the Columbia Association in Columbia, Maryland; the arts reporter and commentator for WJHU, the Baltimore NPR station; and a management and audience development consultant to several arts organizations. He was the founder of the Howard County, Maryland Commission on the Arts. He has produced and promoted a number of art music, and craft festivals and other special events.

In addition to his arts activity, he spent over ten years in academia; teaching at the community college level; serving as the Assistant Director for Community Colleges of the New Jersey Department of Higher Education; and as the Director of Funding and Development for Howard County Community College. As the Executive Director of the non-profit Columbia Forum he was responsible for a three year long community organization project which involved over 5000 citizens in the development of long-term goals for the new town of Columbia. He was the principle author of the "Agenda for Columbia," the final report and recommendations of that agency.

As an account executive for Ruder & Finn Public Relations, his clients included labor unions, international organizations and industry associations. He managed a national speaker's bureau for Ruder & Finn and as a freelance PR consultant developed public relations programs for local arts groups, commercial software firms, and non-profit organizations.

As a freelance writer and consultant he wrote the ground breaking "Report on Weight and Size Discrimination" for the Maryland Human Relations Commission. And, for the Martin Luther King, Jr., Federal Holiday commission he wrote and supervised the design and production of "Living the Dream," the commission's explanation of the new national holiday.

He holds a BA and an MA in History from San Francisco State College and a diploma from the NYU School of Radio and Television. He was a Hopkins Fellow in Organizational and Community Systems. He is the exorbitantly proud father of two remarkable sons.

In the time Bev Sykes has been on CompuServe, she has also worked with The Experiment in International Living (placing foreign students in American homes. She was regional director and on the President's Board). She has been a member and Publicity Director of her local PFLAG (Parents, Friends and Families of Lesbians And Gays.) Bev has worked with her local homeless shelter and Breaking Barriers, which is a social service outreach to HIV infected clients in the Sacramento Area.

Sykes is the publicist for singer/songwriter Steve Schalchlin (and recently wrote the lyrics for a song which will be in a musical that he is debuting in August). Bev is also a theatre critic for our local newspaper, and just recently helped found a group called, I must admit, "Boobs" (Babes on Outrageous Bicycles), which is a group of women on line who are bike riders.

One year for Bev's birthday, I wrote a silly song that ended "And how old are you?" The staff members insisted that she answer the question but I told them I already knew how old she was and gave them an age but I had converted the number to another numerical system and would not tell which system I had used. Bob Mitchell asked "Fahrenheit to Centigrade?" We often have fun in the staff section. Bev has been with us in the Internet family circle for almost as long as Dave Tucker.

Dorr Altizer has been webmaster in all of my forums for almost five years. Although Dorr was born (in 1947) and raised in Huntington, West Virginia, home of the C&O Railroad's Huntington Locomotive Shops, he has only been an active model railroader and railfan since 1970. He had a rewarding career in the U.S. Air Force and retired in 1990 after 25 years. It was the Air Force's decision to station him in the Upper Peninsula of Michigan that began his interest in railroads. While working on top of a B-52H in a swirling blizzard he watched a Soo Line GP30 struggling to drag its cars to Sault Ste. Marie. He was hooked!

Dorr is the owner of Tad Lane Creations, a web page design company, and is a member of the Arizona Rail Passenger Association, the National Association of Railroad Passengers, the National Model Railroad Association Layout Design Special Interest Group, the National Railway Historical Society and the Southern Pacific Historical & Technical Society. He's a Life Member of the National Model Railroad Association and a Life Member of their Pacific Southwest Region (PSR). He's also the Editor of the "PSR Dispatch," the official house organ of the PSR. Dorr and his wife Jan (and 5 cats) live in Surprise, Arizona, just west of a siding named Lizard Acres (milepost 171.6) on the BNSF line from Williams to Phoenix. So if you ask him where he lives, he just smiles and says, "Lizard Acres, Arizona."

I met Jim Dellon in Washington, DC when I was there for the Smithsonian award. Jim does an amazing job of enforcing the forum rules and adding interesting information to the discussions. Jim is a Sysop in the Political Debate Forum but he also helped in Issues Forum in earlier days.

Dan Kohanski assists the sponsors of The Scholars' Corner in Religion Forum and helps in other sections when needed. Jean and Dan like to travel, especially in areas where they can meet new people and where their travel will be of some benefit to the locals -

by that I mean that in southern Africa where Jean and Dan visited last year, they specialize in ecological travel, which supports the local economy while trying to have minimal impact on the land and the wildlife.

Dan was raised in the Jewish tradition and studied Talmud, and he keeps up his interest in the history of Judaism in particular and western religion in general - primarily Christianity but also Islam. His theological position, based on his studies and his readings of history, is that whatever it is that is out there, NO religion, east or west, has got it right as of yet. (And it may even be that the right answer, if there is one, is beyond mankind's grasp.) And too often religion becomes an excuse to feel superior and a justification for evil actions. But insofar as religion provides spiritual comfort and direction, it does have value regardless of whether it got the details correct. Dan is an author - that is, he has one non-fiction book published and is trying to sell a novel (fantasy.)

Jon Dainty is an American Baptist minister who is active in northeast Ohio in ecumenical relations. He is also an amateur radio operator, call sign NM0O, and was licensed in 1979. He and his wife Karen enjoy bowling, NASCAR auto racing, figure skating, and their nieces. Jon is father to Jon, Jr., a soldier at Fort Campbell, KY, and grandfather to Catherine, born in 1999. Computer communications keep him in touch and off the streets. Jon is a Sysop in the Fellowship Forum.

Nate Lenow says he is a member of too many professional associations and he has been elected as an officer in some of these and served on many committees. Nate has been active in local civic groups and in state and local government projects. He was a Sysop in the White House Forum and now serves in Political Debate Forum. When time permits Nate writes articles for professional publications.

Aisha Musa has been our expert on Islam for almost a decade. She is working on her doctoral dissertation in Muslim history and has taught at Harvard.

Jacquie Koplen has been our expert on Judaism for over a decade. She is very knowledgeable on controversial issues involving the Jews. She has been teaching at a nearby school since her physician husband retired.

Kevin Casey has been a staff member in Political Debate Forum for a few years and he is doing a remarkable job in some of the most difficult sections. Kevin remains cool and polite at times Toots would say "Would make a preacher swear." Kevin is also a lot of fun. Here is his description of himself and, although I can't verify the physical attributes, I agree with the rest. <Smile> "I'm tall, and stunningly good looking. In addition, I'm brilliant and articulate. Please describe me accurately. <Grin>"

Kristi Harding lives with her husband, five children, dog (Jess), cat (Whitie), two fish (Beta and Stein), and hermit crab (Chompers). They hike the Carolina mountains and have completed a few week long backpacking trips. The kids keep her on the run. She loves mysteries and is still trying to solve the "Mystery of the Missing Socks". In her "spare time", Kristi teaches physically disabled middle school students. She enjoys witnessing their joy as they meet new challenges. She has learned much from her students. Kristi has been a member of Fellowship Forum since the fall of 1995 and a Sysop there for over five years. She has fun making friends around the world.

Hal Portner is a certified and experienced K-12 teacher and administrator. He was Assistant Director of the Summer Math Program for High School Women and Teachers, Mount Holyoke College, and for 14 years, was a teacher and administrator in a Connecticut public school district. He holds a M.Ed. from the University of Michigan, a 6th year CAGS in Education Administration from the University of Connecticut, and for three years was with the University of Massachusetts Ed.D. Educational Leadership Program. From 1985 to 1995, Hal was on the staff of the Connecticut State Department of Education, Bureau of Certification and Professional Development, where he worked closely with school districts to develop and carry out professional development and teacher evaluation plans and programs. Among the major accomplishments of the Bureau was the development, implementation, and fine-tuning of Connecticut's Beginning Educator Support and Training (BEST) program, a nationally acclaimed beginning teacher mentoring and assessment initiative.

His book Mentoring New Teachers is published by Corwin Press (an affiliate of Sage Publications). Hal now writes, consults and presents workshops for educational organizations and institutions. He currently serves (one day per week) as Consultant for Professional Development for the faculty and staff of a Community College in Massachusetts where, among other responsibilities, he works with the professional development committee and trains experienced faculty members to be Mentors. Hal manages the Teacher Development section in The Education Forum and gives general Sysop assistance.

Cheri Evans has been an educator her entire adult life. She has taught in many areas of the profession from General Education through CDB (EMH), CDS (TMH), LD Primary and Intermediate, both self-contained and resource room. The period in General Education classes was in preparation for obtaining her certification in Educational Leadership. She wanted to "round out" her resume as her goal was to be a Principal or Supervisor of Special Education - a goal she has now attained. New goal: Director of Special Education! During those years in General Education, Cheri taught a first-third multi-age class, a first-second split, a fourth-fifth-sixth grade TAG class and second graders. Cheri returned to the field of Special Education as a CDS (EMH) teacher in a middle school. She is currently an administrator in Wisconsin. She is Special Education Supervisor for eight schools in our southern region. She supervises those schools and 45+ staff members across all exceptionalities, including Gifted Ed TAG. In the evenings she has taught ESL classes at a community college and citizenship classes through the YWCA. Cheri manages the gifted and talented education section and assists with general Sysop work.

Veronica Ugulano leads Section 6, Students/Home/Alt. and assists in all forum areas. Armed with "only" a high school education, Veronica has taken on the project of home schooling her son who is currently in high school. This has brought her closer to various educational opportunities such as nature studies, computer hardware and software, graphics design and web design. In addition, she is currently working privately as a remedial reading teacher.

A few years ago I made a comment about the Pied Piper (of

Hamlin) and then I realized we had a Piper named Bill but he had not been pied yet (or looked as colourful as "pied" suggests). The staffers started suggesting various kinds of pie to throw at poor Bill and we had a lot of fun with that. Bill has been leader for various topics over the years and is doing the Hate Debate section in Political Debate Forum now.

Roselle (Mooosie) Weiner began her on-line leadership career in The Issues Forum in The Village Elders section. When that section moved to Debate Forum and combined with 50+ issues Roselle was the logical leader. She is a lot of fun at her work and inserts funny comments into her messages. I was instructing the staff one day and told them not to call the members "whiners" unless they meant Roselle and could not spell her last name. I did not escape with that pun. In "real life", Mooosie is in library work.

Pamela Troy first started on Compuserve back in the '80s, on the religion forum. At the time religion interested her strongly, mainly because she'd been following the rise of the religious right since she was in college. For a few years she dropped off, then returned in about 1995, this time concentrating on the political forum, perhaps because the religious right had mainstreamed itself to the point where it could be easily discussed in that context. Her interests that involve this forum are propaganda, church and state, history, and logic.

Troy manages the Civil Society section, which fits in with her interest in the rise of irrationality in public debate. She's especially interested in the way language is used - or misused - to promote a political agenda.

Back in the summer of 2001, she read a tongue-in-cheek essay by Podvin, in which he asked exactly what would be the reaction if, in 2004, G.W. Bush called off the presidential election. He was referring to the fact that Bush so far had gotten pretty much anything he wanted from congress, the Supreme Court, etc. Was ANYONE ever going to say "no" to this guy? Pamela thought it was a thought-provoking question so, in about the first week of September, she posted the same question - what if Bush were to call off the 2004 presidential election? - to the political forum (referencing Podvin).

One evening - September 10 - she looked over the responses she'd gotten, and composed a reply to one of her respondents. He had said in answer to her question, "Well, the states would hold elections anyway, and the country would elect a Democratic Congress (if they had not already done so in the '02 election) and the congress would impeach, and convict Il Deuce and remove him from office on the grounds that he had violated his specific oath of office and committed a 'high crime.'" That quieted some, but not Pamela.

She typed out the following response:

> "That's assuming that we haven't gone to war by then, or suffered a massive economic crash, or some other state of emergency. If we go to war, bringing up Bush's legitimacy as president - indeed, even questioning his policies - could very well be denounced as disloyal. In an atmosphere where, as she's observed, the rhetoric about liberals is already bellicose and borderline violent, things could get very, VERY nasty."

Then she looked over it, decided it needed some polishing, and resolved to sleep on it, do a rewrite, and shoot the response off to the board the following afternoon. Which was September 11, 2001. Sigh.

Troy did send the message PRIVATELY a little later that week. It didn't seem right to post it to the public board after what had happened in New York that morning. It's the only time in her life where she's clamped her mouth shut on a social issue because she thought what she was saying might be too close to the truth.

After a 27-year, lucrative career in the entertainment business, as an audio/lighting engineer, Randy Todd was diagnosed with advanced Type II diabetes, while undergoing emergency surgery for removal of his gall bladder. He was rudely awakened by the cost of medical treatment and maintenance of this chronic ailment, which affects nearly 16 million Americans. He took it upon myself to become an advocate for those who cannot afford the ever-increasing cost of pharmaceutical drugs, doctors and medical insurance.

In 1995, Todd was recruited by the Sysop of the White House Forum as a Section Leader. Surviving the subsequent sale of CompuServe to AOL, Todd was transferred to the Political Debate Forum during the reformation period.

Bob Mitchell is a chemical engineer who has been married to a registered nurse for 31 years. They have three talented children - a daughter who is a teacher, a daughter who is a doctor and a son just finishing a degree in mechanical engineering. The Mitchells have lived on the Gulf Coast for 22 years. I sometimes think of Bob as our forum clown, or one of them anyway. Staff members were teasing Dave Tucker about his age and Bob said he could not handle such large numbers. I assured Dave that I was a couple years older than he was so he should not worry about those numbers. Bob works in the "We the People" section of The Political Debate Forum where much of the controversy is posted.

Al Goggins, who leads the education and parents section in Political Debate Forum and assists in the financial section, has been with us since early White House Forum days. He is a C.P.A. (Certified Public Accountant) and an I.R.S. Agent - specifically, an International Examiner in what used to be the Coordinated Exam Program at the time that White House Forum was formed (which has been changed to the Large and Mid-Sized Business program). He primarily audits the international activities of multinational corporations. His opinions and commentary are strictly his own and do not represent his employer. "I graduated from U.C. Berkeley, class of '68, and all that goes with that. <G>," he says. (<G> is email shorthand for "big grin".)

Jack Douglass retired after 29 years with the Fresno County Juvenile Probation Department several years ago where he supervised Juvenile Hall counselors and ran programs within that facility. He moved into a neighborhood with at-risk youth and immersed himself in full-time ministry through Youth for Christ and Baptist Temple, the Fellowship of Joy. At the present time, Jack is Director of Community and Equipping Ministries for Baptist Temple and develops ministers to work with adults and youth in the inner city. He recently married DeAnn Dominie and is the father of two children and grandfather of more. He still teaches juvenile hall counselors through the community college and is a respected leader of the community in Fresno, California. Jack assists in the Fellowship Forum.

We have several staff members from the UK among them Chris Eyre who assists the sponsors of the Christianity section in the Religion Forum, manages the multilingual section and assists with other sections. Jill Seal assists the sponsor of the Social Hall section and Richard Waterfield manages the Worship section in the Fellowship Forum.

Our two newest section leaders are doing a fine job. Mike Haggerty leads the Firearms Debate section in Political Debate Forum and is teased about playing with guns in the shooting gallery. Allan Kempe was not sure he wanted to try staff work but he is doing such a fine job in three Debate sections that it would have been a shame if he had not been convinced that he could handle the duties. Allan is managing the Republican Debate, Rush Limbaugh and Media sections.

No Sysop could do all of this work alone and I am deeply grateful for the fine, dedicated help of all my staff members.

CHAPTER 10

Full Circle: memories' back in their boxes

Toots always said "I can do anything but be the father of a large family." To that I add, "I can't sing bass." We are all limited in some way and we should not blame the rest of the world for our limitations. I have read that everyone has a handicap or disability, some show and some don't. In the past children have stopped Toots and me on the street and said "I want to see her eyes." After looking at me closely they say "She doesn't look blind." True, I don't "look blind" but of course looking like a sighted person does not make me see any better. My optic nerve was atrophied at birth, not my eyes.

A young Georgia and her mother, Toots.

I have always said that society owes us nothing unless we do our part; that if all a person can do is smile and she sits with a glum look on her face, society owes her nothing. We receive what we are willing to give.

I have always felt that if I notice something wrong in the world and do not do whatever I can to make it better, it is just as much my fault as anyone else's. There are people who will try to take advantage of this willingness to help but we soon learn to distinguish real needs.

Blind people are just like other groups - some are endowed with what seems like extra skills or intelligence while others seem limited. We should never judge an individual based on generalities for a group. If someone says "Isn't that just like a woman?" ask "Which woman? Lizzie Borden or Mother Teresa?" (Lizzie Borden was a mentally imbalanced murderer famous for giving Father "40 whacks" and Mother "40 more", and Mother Teresa was a charitable, kind, and loving person.) Just as snowflakes are all different so humans are not alike. Each of us has some talent that should be given major attention and improved. Although having a role model is often a good start we need to be realistic about choosing that model. None of us should aim to be a carbon copy of someone else and how well do you think a monotone would fare trying to emulate a famous singer?

Find your talents and work at them so that you can contribute something special to this world. It does not have to be something major to be worthy of attention. After all, every good link in a chain makes that chain stronger.

I don't feel that I have done anything in my life that others cannot do if they really want to do those things. I have simply done what I had to do to survive and live a happy life and carry on the circles of loving family and friends. When I started writing this book I promised that I would behave like a modern washer, when I spin dry I'll automatically shut myself off. That time has come. All dry. Goodbye!